History of Egypt

An Enthralling Overview of Egyptian History

Free limited time bonus

Stop for a moment. We have a free bonus set up for you. The problem is this: we forget 90% of everything that we read after 7 days. Crazy fact, right? Here's the solution: we've created a printable, 1-page pdf summary for this book that you're reading now. All you have to do to get your free pdf summary is to go to the following website: **https://livetolearn.lpages.co/enthrallinghistory/**

Once you do, it will be intuitive. Enjoy, and thank you!

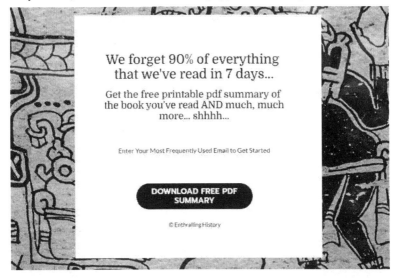

We forget 90% of everything that we've read in 7 days...

Get the free printable pdf summary of the book you've read AND much, much more... shhhh...

Enter Your Most Frequently Used Email to Get Started

DOWNLOAD FREE PDF SUMMARY

© Enthralling History

Contents

INTRODUCTION 1

PART ONE: AN OVERVIEW OF ANCIENT EGYPT (3150–330 BCE) 4

CHAPTER 1: THE START OF ANCIENT EGYPT (3150–2180 BCE) 5

CHAPTER 2: THE MIDDLE KINGDOM EMERGES
(2180–1550 BCE) 17

CHAPTER 3: THE NEW KINGDOM (1550–1070 BCE) 29

CHAPTER 4: THE END OF ANCIENT EGYPT (1070–330 BCE) 43

PART TWO: AN OVERVIEW OF MODERN EGYPT
(332 BCE–2021 CE) 54

CHAPTER 5: THE GRECO-ROMAN PERIOD (332 BCE–629 CE) 55

CHAPTER 6: MEDIEVAL EGYPT (650–1520 CE) 67

CHAPTER 7: EARLY MODERN EGYPT (1520–1914 CE) 78

CHAPTER 8: LATE MODERN EGYPT (1890–2013 CE) 91

PART THREE: EGYPTIAN SOCIETY THROUGH THE AGES 103

CHAPTER 9: SOCIETY AND ITS STRUCTURE 104

CHAPTER 10: THE NILE AND ITS KEY ROLE 115

CHAPTER 11: THE DEVELOPMENT OF RELIGION 125

CHAPTER 12: LANGUAGE, ART, AND ARCHITECTURE 135

PART FOUR: KEY FIGURES IN EGYPTIAN HISTORY 147

CHAPTER 13: TUTANKHAMUN AND HIS CURSED TOMB
(1341–1327 BC) 148

CHAPTER 14: HATSHEPSUT AND CLEOPATRA: WOMEN IN POWER 161

CHAPTER 15: SALADIN: THE FIRST SULTAN OF EGYPT 172

CHAPTER 16: MUBARAK AND MORSI.. 180

CONCLUSION 191

HERE'S ANOTHER BOOK BY ENTHRALLING HISTORY THAT YOU MIGHT LIKE... 193

FREE LIMITED TIME BONUS 194

BIBLIOGRAPHY:... 195

Introduction

Egypt is a vibrant country that draws millions of visitors every year. People from all over the world flock to the home of the pharaohs to tour the Nile and visit its historic landmarks. While it is a beautiful country with a fascinating blend of cultures, much of its allure is due to its illustrious and enigmatic history. From magnificent palaces to towering pyramids, Egypt's history is part of the landscape, which allows it to fit seamlessly into Egypt's bright present and future. However, the country is so much more than a handful of old pyramids and temples. This book will take the reader on a comprehensive tour of Egypt's ancient, medieval, and modern history, which will deepen your appreciation for this magnificent country.

Part one of this book provides a brief but comprehensive overview of ancient Egypt and the powerful dynasties that ruled over it. Discover how Lower and Upper Egypt became a country that produced stunning works of art. These dynasties formed an integral part of the Egyptian empire. The kings were associated with the divine and ruled with iron fists. Learn about some of the most important kings and what they did with their godly kingships.

The second part of this book leaves pharaohs and pyramids behind. It picks up from the Greek and Roman takeover, which ended independent Egyptian rule and introduced new ruling dynasties and cultures. For example, the Ptolemaic kingdom was a unique Greco-Egyptian ruling family with a dramatic history that has been the subject of books, films, and art for centuries. However, there's more to this period than over-the-top rulers, as the Nile became a key port that generated trade for the country. During this time, Egypt became a center of philosophy and attracted famous scholars. In time, Egypt became a Muslim country and had to fight fiercely for its independence.

The next section will discuss Egyptian society through the ages. From ancient to modern times, the structure of society has contributed to how the country functioned. This section will examine factors like the Nile River and how it impacted society and the economy. It will also take a look at religion, art, architecture, and language, which all had an immeasurable impact on the country as a whole.

Finally, the last chapters of the book will be dedicated to taking a look at some of the most important figures in Egyptian history. Find out about the boy king, Tutankhamun, who ruled for a few short years and whose unexpected death ensured his lasting legacy. The story of his cursed tomb has been a subject of fascination for years and opened up a larger conversation about the preservation of Egyptian treasures. While Egypt was mostly ruled by men, there were women who managed to rule in their own right, such as Hatshepsut and Cleopatra.

In time, the Age of Pharaohs passed, and the Greeks and Romans lost control of the area, which allowed sultans to take power. Discover the story of Saladin, Egypt's first sultan who ushered in a period of great change for the country. Ancient Egypt's political system was larger than life and fraught with danger, but modern Egypt's politics are no less intriguing. Find out more about Hosni Mubarak and Mohammed Morsi, who were both Egyptian presidents who faced monumental challenges during their time in office.

Egyptian history is so much more than its ancient period, and that's something this book sets out to prove. Some of the most fundamental events in Egypt's illustrious history have been laid out in a simple format that allows the reader to discover Egypt's secrets without causing them to lose interest or get lost in a maze of scholarly descriptions. Reading this book is like taking a leisurely tour through Egypt's glittering history and will provide an overview of Egypt's impact on the world in general.

Egypt is one of the most beautiful countries in the world, and its history only adds to its allure. Allow this book to deepen your understanding and appreciation for the home of the pharaohs.

PART ONE: An Overview of Ancient Egypt (3150–330 BCE)

Chapter 1: The Start of Ancient Egypt (3150–2180 BCE)

The Egyptian empire was around for centuries and experienced several periods of significant changes. This makes it difficult to keep track of Egypt's history, which is why historians group ancient Egyptian history into different kingdoms and intermediate periods. A dynasty in ancient Egyptian history refers to rulers who shared ancestors or origins. There were thirty-two commonly accepted pharaonic dynasties. The earliest of these periods was the Early Dynastic Period, which began soon after Upper and Lower Egypt were united. Next came the Old Kingdom, which is also known as the Age of Pyramids. During this era, the great Egyptian kings built the famous pyramids that still draw visitors to Egypt.

Before Egypt was a prosperous empire, the region consisted of various Neolithic societies that settled along the banks of the Nile. The river provided these communities with everything they needed to thrive. In time, these societies formed kingdoms that became known as Upper and Lower Egypt. These two kingdoms frequently fought each other. Their rivalry became legendary and may have formed the basis of one of Egypt's most enduring myths. However, the kingdoms were eventually united under one ruler, the legendary Menes, who formed the foundation of the Egyptian empire.

Neolithic Egyptian Societies

For thousands of years, Neolithic communities lived along the banks of the Nile and built a comfortable life for themselves. During the period between 9300 and 4000 BCE, Egypt was the home to a diverse group of people who aren't well known because evidence of their existence has been covered by floodplains or the surrounding desert. Thousands of years ago, the regions that are now arid desert plains were once lush and fertile lands. Those conditions attracted Neolithic farmers to raise their crops and flocks in Egypt. Not much is known about these people since they haven't been studied as extensively as their successors, but some burial and ancient sites have shed light on these mysterious tribes.

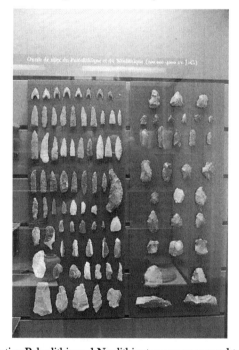

Egyptian Paleolithic and Neolithic stone weapons and tools.
Gary Todd from Xinzheng, China, CC0, via Wikimedia Commons;
https://commons.wikimedia.org/wiki/File:Ancient_Egypt_Paleolithic_%26_Neolithic_Ston
e_Weapons_%26_Tools_(28426678975).jpg

Historians have found evidence of megaliths, calendar circles, and shrines, which indicate that the Neolithic people practiced elaborate and distinct religions. In time, these Neolithic tribes began developing funerary rites and buried their dead in dedicated cemeteries. Archaeologists found pottery, shells, jewelry, tools, and weapons buried with the dead. Some of these cemeteries revealed surprising secrets. A few cemeteries were found with people in their fifties, which was an impressive age for the time, but Egypt is also home to the world's oldest discovered infant cemetery, which contained women with their infants, late-term fetuses, and babies.

These grave sites have allowed historians to pull back the curtains of time, as they contain numerous clues about the people buried in them. For example, it is clear that these Neolithic communities had rigid social structures since the grave sites containing older people likely belonged to the elite, while the graves containing younger people might have belonged to poorer workers. These cultures may have practiced polygamy, and families were likely buried together. Great respect was shown to the dead, which may have contributed to later beliefs about the dead. It's clear that while the early Neolithic settlers of ancient Egypt are mostly lost to history, they had a clear impact on the people who later populated Egypt. In time, these tribes formed into two distinct kingdoms: Upper and Lower Egypt.

Upper Egypt

The region that made up the area of Upper Egypt spanned from Cairo to Lake Nasser. It was also known as the Land of Reeds and included all the lands between the Nile and Nubia. For hundreds of years, the capital city of Upper Egypt was Nekhen, which was the patron city of the vulture-like goddess Nekhbet. When the two kingdoms were united, she became the patron goddess of the entire region, elevating her status from a local goddess to a more influential deity.

The people who lived in Upper Egypt before the unification were mostly farmers and herders. They grew emmer, lentils, sesame, wheat, barley, and papyrus. In time, Upper Egypt produced crops like garlic, sugarcane, onions, lettuce, and chickpeas. The land was fertile thanks to the Nile, which meant that the people had more than enough to eat. The Nile was an integral part of their lives, as its flooding allowed the land to remain fertile and prevented their lands from turning into desert plains.

During this time, people began developing distinctive pottery and worked with copper. They also began making mudbricks similar to the ones used in Mesopotamia and used recessed walls and arches in their buildings. These decorative elements were impressive for the time and would have led to the development of more decorative architectural techniques. The people of Upper Egypt were accustomed to warfare since they frequently engaged in battles against Lower Egypt.

Lower Egypt

Lower Egypt was made up of the Nile River delta region that ran to the Mediterranean Sea. You might have figured this out already, but the Nile runs south to north, unlike most rivers. The delta region was famously well watered thanks to several channels and canals that branched off from the Nile, making vast pieces of land incredibly fertile. The capital city of Lower Egypt was the city of Memphis, which was the patron city of the goddess Wadjet. This goddess was often represented as a cobra. Eventually, the two kingdoms were unified, and the two goddesses, Wadjet and Nekhbet, were often pictured together and became known as the Two Ladies.

While the two kingdoms were eventually unified, they still had distinct cultures that shared some similarities but were ultimately unique. These distinct cultures were represented by the Pschent or double crown of Egypt, which the ruler wore. The crown consisted of the Hedjet, which was the white crown that represented Upper

Egypt, and the Deshret, which was the red crown that represented Lower Egypt. The union of the two kingdoms became a common theme in Egyptian iconography. Some of these images depicted the goddesses Wadjet and Nekhbet, while others showed the gods Horus and Seth knotting papyrus and reed plants, which represented the two kingdoms. The two separate kingdoms rose to prominence during the last stage of prehistoric Egypt, and their unification would mark a new era. The ancient Egyptians accredited the unification of the two kingdoms to Menes, who has been identified by historians as King Narmer.

King Narmer

The unification of Upper and Lower Egypt was a triumphant feat that had long been accredited to a man named Menes. For years, historians accepted that Menes rose to the challenge of unifying the two kingdoms, but this became difficult since they couldn't locate his rule in the historical record. Another problem was that Menes was simply an honorific, meaning "he who endures." Eventually, historians concluded that Menes was likely King Narmer, whom historians believed ruled shortly before the unification. They surmised that Narmer was known as Menes after he unified the regions, and there is evidence of him wearing the crowns of both Upper and Lower Egypt, which gives credence to this theory.

King Narmer carved into a slate palette.
https://commons.wikimedia.org/wiki/File:EB1911_Egypt_-_Early_Art_-_King_Narmer,_Slate_Palette.jpg

If this is true, then Narmer was the first king of Egypt. Historians believe that Narmer originated in Upper Egypt and came from the city of Thinis. He began conquering the states around his kingdom before moving on to Lower Egypt. Some believe that he peacefully took over Lower Egypt, although the Narmer Palette, an artifact containing some of the earliest hieroglyphs in the region, depicts Narmer as a mighty warrior. Whatever means were used, Narmer managed to unify Upper and Lower Egypt around 3150 BCE.

For years, Upper Egypt had been rapidly developing into a more urban civilization that traded with other cultures, while Lower Egypt was somewhat more rural, which may have helped the unification. Narmer seems to have been a good king who ruled peacefully. When he died, it's possible that his wife, Neithhotep, may have ruled for some time since her tomb was elaborate and showed that she enjoyed significant status during her life.

The Rivalry between Horus and Seth

In the ancient Egyptian religion, Horus was a god who was represented by a falcon. His right eye represented the sun and power, while the left eye represented the moon and healing. He was often mentioned in connection with the god Seth, with the two being presented as mortal enemies. Seth was a trickster god with various animal features. He was known as the god of the desert, warfare, and chaos. Seth and Horus's reconciliation provided the mythical basis for the unification of Lower and Upper Egypt. Pharaohs were eventually thought to be the living representations of Horus and wore dual crowns that symbolized the unity between the two regions.

Carving depicting Horus defeating Seth.
Karen Green, CC BY-SA 2.0 https://creativecommons.org/licenses/by-sa/2.0 , via Wikimedia Commons; https://commons.wikimedia.org/wiki/File:Flickr_-_schmuela_-_Horus_defeats_Seth.jpg

The myth centers on Osiris, Isis, Horus, and Seth. According to the myth, Osiris was the king of Egypt and a descendant of the creator god Ra. His queen was Isis, who gave the women of Egypt the gifts of weaving, beer brewing, and baking. The couple was very happy and ruled Egypt in harmony. Osiris was also associated with power and rightful rulership, which contrasted sharply with Seth's powers. In time, Osiris's brother, Seth, became jealous of him and wanted to claim the kingship for himself. Seth built an ornate wooden chest and coated it in lead. The trickster managed to trap Osiris in the chest and threw it into the Nile.

Osiris died, and in his absence, Seth became king. However, Isis wasn't willing to forget her husband. She searched everywhere for his body. Eventually, she found the wooden chest in the Nile and brought it home. When Seth discovered what Isis had done, he hacked Osiris's body into pieces and scattered them all over the world. Isis and her sister, Nephthys, tracked down all the pieces and put Osiris back together with bandages. Unfortunately, Osiris's penis was missing, but Isis used magic to make her husband whole again. However, he was neither living nor dead and became the first mummy. Nine months later, Isis bore a son and named him Horus.

When Horus was old enough, he challenged Seth since he was the rightful ruler of Egypt. Seth and Horus fought, and in the bloody battle, Horus's left eye became damaged. This formed an explanation for the phases of the moon. Horus and Seth fought on multiple occasions, but in time, they were reconciled.

King Djoser and Imhotep

King Djoser became the king of Egypt around 2650 BCE and is known for his great building projects, including Egypt's first pyramid. He was the first king of the Third Dynasty (although some sources claim that he was the second) and began commissioning building projects almost as soon as he took the throne. His reign saw great innovations in architecture, including the advancement of designs, symbolism, and ornamentations. Djoser secured Egypt's borders, and Egypt was stable for most of his reign, which lasted about two decades. His tomb, the Step Pyramid of Saqqara, was built under the direction of his vizier, Imhotep, and was the tallest building in the world at that time.

Statue of Imhotep.
Cstew1996, CC0, via Wikimedia Commons;
https://commons.wikimedia.org/wiki/File:Imhotep8.jpg

While Djoser was a good king, much of his success stemmed from the capabilities of his vizier, the famed Imhotep. After Imhotep died, he was deified and became the god of medicine and wisdom. During his lifetime, Imhotep was an accomplished poet, polymath, physician, architect, and astronomer. While he is best known for overseeing Djoser's Step Pyramid, he also wrote treatises about disease and injury that advanced the field of medicine at the time. He may have started out as a priest but quickly rose through the ranks to become one of the most important men in Egypt.

Under his direction, the Step Pyramid rose to about sixty-two meters high and included a complex that housed a temple, shrines, courtyards, and a living space for the priests. It included many important religious symbols and drew travelers from all over.

King Sneferu

King Sneferu was the first king of the Fourth Dynasty and began ruling around 2575 BCE. His reign proved to be the peak of the Old Kingdom, and he refined the art of pyramid-building. Sneferu ushered in a golden age and built two pyramids at Dahshur. His pyramid at Meidum is referred to as the "false pyramid" because it rests on a huge heap of soil and resembles a tower instead of a pyramid. While the pyramid was undoubtedly impressive, it eventually collapsed sometime after it was built since its foundation was made out of sand instead of rock. It's likely that the builders used Imhotep's original design but made a few modifications that led to its collapse.

Sneferu was known for being a competent king who managed to stabilize his country and win many battles against Nubia and Libya. He built several pyramids, including the Red Pyramid, which is Egypt's first true pyramid. (A "true" pyramid is one with smooth sides, not stepped sides.) Sneferu's earlier attempts fell short of his goal, but he didn't stop until he created the perfect pyramid. While he commissioned many projects, his country didn't suffer because of his ambitions, and Egypt remained stable under his reign.

The Pyramids of Giza

Thanks to King Sneferu's efforts, his successors had the blueprints to build true and lasting pyramids. As a result, the next three kings built the famous Pyramids of Giza. Khufu succeeded Sneferu on the throne. The Greeks considered him a tyrant who abused his power. According to their records, he forced his people into slavery. Herodotus claimed that Khufu introduced various evils to his kingdom and conscripted hundreds of thousands of men to work without pay on his pyramid. He also claimed that the unscrupulous ruler forced his own daughter to work in brothels to raise money for his project. However, Egyptian sources state that he was a good king who took care of his workers and only hired men during times when farming wasn't possible due to the Nile flooding.

Khafre later built his pyramid alongside Khufu's and may have commissioned the Sphinx since the Sphinx's face closely resembles his own. Like Khufu, the Greeks remembered Khafre as an oppressive tyrant, but there isn't much evidence left from his reign to refute the claims. He was succeeded by his son, Menkaure, who built his own temple complex at Giza and was praised by both the Greeks and Egyptians. Unfortunately, it seems that Egypt's abundant resources had begun to dwindle under the weight of such massive building projects, and Menkaure's complex was somewhat smaller than his predecessors' tombs.

The Fifth and Sixth Dynasties

One of King Sneferu's lasting acts was to ally his kingship with the cult of the god Ra. One of his successors, Djedefre, claimed that Egyptian kings were the sons of Ra instead of the living embodiment of Ra. This act allowed Egyptian priests to become increasingly powerful, which diminished the kingship considerably. During the Fifth Dynasty, a woman named Khentkaus became incredibly important, and her tomb is the fourth pyramid at Giza, although no one is quite sure why she received such a high honor. The kings of the Fifth Dynasty are known as the Sun Kings because many of them had names that were derived from the sun god Ra.

Unfortunately, the kingship was slowly losing power as administrators became increasingly more powerful. The Sixth Dynasty began with the rule of Teti, who was murdered by his own men. Government officials dared to build grand tombs that rivaled those of the noble classes. Pepi II Neferkare was a notable king during this period; the texts from the time say he ruled for almost a hundred years and was a capable king at first. However, the longer Pepi II ruled, the more unstable the kingdom became. Egypt needed a powerful and energetic king, but Pepi II grew old and lacked the zeal to make a difference. The central government became increasingly destabilized, and he outlived many of his possible successors. Soon after he died, the Sixth Dynasty ended, as did the Old Kingdom.

The First Intermediate Period

In ancient Egyptian history, there were many periods of prosperity and stability, as well as times of instability. The times of stability are known as kingdoms, while the times of instability are known as intermediate periods. The Old Kingdom ended around 2181 BCE, and the First Intermediate Period began. During this time, Egypt's central government collapsed and was almost completely ineffectual. This allowed local administrators to take care of their own areas. For many years, those officials had been gathering power at the government's expense. Egyptian districts had been divided into nomes by previous kings, and these administrators were known as nomarchs. The nomarchs became incredibly rich and built lavish homes and tombs for themselves.

A terrible drought caused conditions to worsen, and the royal family struggled to come up with a suitable heir when Pepi II died. The First Intermediate Period was characterized by disunity, including friction between Upper and Lower Egypt. It was a time of immense change. There aren't any significant monuments from this era, and art suffered somewhat. There are few written records from this period, which led many to believe that it was a time of chaos. However, it appears that rural areas became richer and more complex during this time. Without a king to use their resources on monuments, the people were able to redirect their resources to other pursuits.

It was certainly a dark age for the social elite of Egypt, as the old order simply didn't matter anymore. However, the lower classes were able to afford more luxury goods, which led to the mass production of many items that had previously been reserved for the higher classes. In time, the kings of Egypt were able to bring the First Intermediate Period to an end and introduced the Middle Kingdom. The First Intermediate Period had a definite effect on Egyptian history, and the Middle Kingdom differed from the Old Kingdom in a few significant ways. For example, the kings of the Middle Kingdom worked with the nomarchs, which stabilized Egypt and turned it into one of the most impressive empires in history.

Chapter 2: The Middle Kingdom Emerges (2180–1550 BCE)

The Middle Kingdom is also known as the Period of Reunification. The First Intermediate Period was a time characterized by political division, as local nomarchs gathered power for themselves. During this time, the monarchy suffered greatly and often didn't have the resources to care for the rest of the kingdom. As a result, local nomarchs (government officials in charge of nomes or territorial divisions within Egypt) stepped up to take care of their territories, which increased their influence. While the aristocracy saw this time as a period of chaos and lawlessness, ordinary people began making more money, and mass production became widespread.

However, fewer significant strides were made in art and architecture. When the First Intermediate Period ended, it was followed by the Middle Kingdom, which is known as Egypt's Classical Age due to the art that was produced during the era. Historians disagree about when the Middle Kingdom began. Some consider the Eleventh Dynasty as the beginning of the Middle Kingdom, while others regard the Twelfth Dynasty as the founders.

One thing is for certain, Mentuhotep II of the Eleventh Dynasty laid the foundation for Egypt's classical period, which would raise Egypt to new heights.

Mentuhotep II

During the First Intermediate Period, Egypt was divided into Upper and Lower Egypt again. Herakleopolis was the most important city in Lower Egypt, while Thebes rose to become the most powerful city in Upper Egypt. Once again, the two kingdoms fought each other for supreme control. The old kings of Egypt tried to retain control from their place of power in Memphis, but their efforts were futile once the priests and nomarchs gathered power for themselves. In time, the monarchy moved to Herakleopolis in an effort to consolidate its power, but it was too little, too late.

Mentuhotep II.
https://commons.wikimedia.org/wiki/File:Mentuhotep_II_(detail).jpg

The depth to which the Egyptian monarchy had sunk became clear when a nomarch named Intef rebelled against traditional authority around 2125 BCE. The monarchy was unable to subdue him, and he set up Thebes as an important power in the region. Egypt was on track for reunification, with Intef's successors building up Theban prestige and power. One of Intef's successors, Wahankh Intef (Intef II), claimed the title of "King of Upper and Lower Egypt." However, it was Mentuhotep II who would unify Egypt. Mentuhotep II conquered other nomes and brought them under his rule. He then conquered Herakleopolis and rival nomarchs who were a threat. As a result, he reunited Upper and Lower Egypt into one kingdom.

Finally, Egypt had a strong central government again, which led to more building projects, art, and military expeditions. During the First Intermediate Period, Egypt's nomes developed distinct cultures and unique traits that would eventually influence Egyptian culture as a whole. Mentuhotep was a competent ruler who focused on strengthening his government, expanding trade, and commissioning various building projects. Mentuhotep built a grand temple and mortuary complex (where he was buried) close to his beloved city of Thebes and died around 1957 BCE. Thanks to his efforts, he left Egypt as a strong and wealthy country and was given the honor of being known as the second "Menes" of Egypt.

The Eleventh Dynasty

Mentuhotep II was a strong king who focused much of his attention on reconquering old territories that had been lost to Egypt since the fall of the Old Kingdom. He also reestablished the idea that Egyptian kings were extensions of the gods. He often wore the headdresses of Amun-Ra (god of the sun and air) and Min (god of fertility and harvest and the Egyptian masculine ideal). These would have been extremely effective ways to strengthen his own power since the people were less likely to question the authority of a god.

Mentuhotep ruled for about fifty-one years and passed the throne to his son, Mentuhotep III.

Mentuhotep III ruled for a little over a decade and adopted many of his father's policies, which further strengthened Egypt. He built various forts in an effort to protect Egypt from invasions from the east. When Mentuhotep died, he was succeeded by Mentuhotep IV.

Much of the information about the Eleventh Dynasty comes from the Turin List of Kings, which is a papyrus manuscript from the reign of Ramesses II of the Nineteenth Dynasty. It is one of the most detailed records of Egyptian kingship. Not only does it contain the names of the Egyptian kings but also their regnal dates. The papyrus separates the kings into their appropriate dynasties. According to the Turin List, Mentuhotep III was succeeded by seven kingless years. There is little to no evidence about Mentuhotep IV's reign, and his name hasn't been found in several Egyptian king lists. A few inscriptions have been found bearing his name, detailing how he sent his vizier, Amenemhat, to a quarry to retrieve stones for a royal monument.

It appears as though there may have been a civil war during this period and that Amenemhat was victorious since he became Amenemhet I. There isn't a clear record of how Amenemhet became king, but since he wasn't a royal, it is easy to lean toward the theory of a civil war or coup.

Thebes

Thebes was built on the banks of the Nile River and was located in the middle of Upper Egypt, south of the delta. At its peak, the city housed about seventy-five thousand people, which made it the largest city in the world during its time. It was a wealthy city that was the seat of royal power for many years, which likely attracted more inhabitants as well as the social elite. It was also an important religious city since it was the center of worship for Amun-Ra. The Eleventh Dynasty's kings ruled from Thebes, but when Mentuhotep

IV was replaced by Amenemhet I, the Egyptian capital was moved to Iti-tawi. This move may have signaled Amenemhet's desire to distance himself from the previous dynasty.

While Thebes was no longer the capital of the kingdom, it still enjoyed significant influence as a religious center. Senusret I, a king from the Twelfth Dynasty, built a temple dedicated to Amun, which shows that the city still received plenty of attention from the monarchy. During the Middle Kingdom, the city was quite large and had at least two palaces within its boundaries. While Thebes enjoyed significant influence during the Middle Kingdom, it only reached its peak during the New Kingdom when Amun became the principal god.

Amenemhet I

While not much is known about Amenemhet's rise to the throne, it is clear that he was a strong and capable leader. Under his rule, Egypt flourished and interacted with other countries. Amenemhet founded the Twelfth Dynasty, which would rule Egypt for the next two centuries and brought about the distinct culture for which the Middle Kingdom is known. It's possible that Amenemhet moved his capital from Thebes to Iti-tawi to distance himself from the Eleventh Dynasty. However, the new capital was located close to Lisht, which was close to the old capital of Herakleopolis. Iti-tawi was built on fertile plains, which would have allowed it to flourish. This suggests that Amenemhet moved the capital in order to establish his dynasty as completely Egyptian instead of just Theban. The new capital was also placed in a central position, which would have allowed him to rule more effectively and consolidate his power in the country.

Amenemhet also made sure to honor the old capital at Thebes by contributing to Amun's temple. He commissioned various building projects, including fortresses to ward off foreign invaders and a massive pyramid and mortuary complex at Lisht. These buildings resembled the Pyramids of Giza, which shows that

Amenemhet wanted to associate himself with the glory of the Old Kingdom kings and their prosperous reigns.

Around the twentieth year of his reign, around 1918 BCE, Amenemhet I appointed his son, Senusret I, as co-regent. Senusret conducted several military campaigns in the south. It would appear as though Amenemhet I faced political unrest during the end of his reign and may have been assassinated.

Art, Culture, and Government during the Middle Kingdom

During the Old Kingdom, art was commissioned to honor the gods, and literary works were usually reserved for Pyramid Texts, inscriptions, and theological stories. However, literature flourished during the Middle Kingdom, and stories about ordinary people became popular. For example, the "Tale of Sinuhe" tells the story of a man who served Amenemhet I but ran away to become a Bedouin after the assassination of the king. He lived among the Bedouin for years since he feared reprisal from Amenemhet's heir, Senusret, even though Sinuhe was not involved in the king's death. In time, Sinuhe longed to return to his home. He eventually received a pardon from the king, which allowed him to live out his final years among his own people.

Other works posed important questions, such as whether or not there was life after death. Poetry and prose became popular, and stories such as the "Tale of the Shipwrecked Sailor" were developed. Sculptures and paintings focused on depicting daily scenes. Grand buildings were designed to highlight the surrounding landscape, such as Mentuhotep II's mortuary complex.

Middle Kingdom boat carving.

Infrogmation of New Orleans, CC BY 2.0 https://creativecommons.org/licenses/by/2.0 via Wikimedia Commons; https://commons.wikimedia.org/wiki/File:Middle_Kingdom_Ancient_Egyptian_boat_artwork_at_New _Orleans_Museum_of_Art.jpg

During the Middle Kingdom, many kings had double dates on their cartouches, which means it's possible that the kings allowed their chosen successors to rule as co-regents in their final years so there would be no disruption when the king died. It also allowed the successor to learn to be an effective king. This theory hasn't been confirmed, but it seems that quite a few kings appointed their successors during their final years and then appointed these successors to be co-regents. When Mentuhotep II reunited Egypt, he appointed members of his own family to high positions within the government and took considerable power away from the nomarchs. Later kings would follow this example, but many of these kings had good relationships with their nomarchs. In fact, during Senusret II's reign, the nomarchs enjoyed as much prosperity as they had during the First Intermediate Period but at no cost to the monarchy's influence. As a result, the nomarchs were fiercely loyal to their king, which helped Egypt prosper.

The Twelfth Dynasty

Like his father before him, Senusret I wanted to associate his kingship with the Old Kingdom rulers. As soon as he took the throne, he began commissioning building projects that closely resembled the monuments of the Old Kingdom. He also built infrastructure that benefited the whole kingdom. Senusret I managed to increase Egypt's prosperity and awarded officials for their loyalty. He curbed the power of the nomarchs but allowed them to grow wealthier without taking power from the monarchy. As a result, Senusret was able to strengthen his own government without alienating the nomarchs. This peace between the monarchy and the nomarchs allowed Senusret to focus on the military, building projects, agriculture, and art.

It would appear as though Senusret I allowed his successor, Amenemhat II, to rule as co-regent alongside him during the last years of his reign. Not much is known about Amenemhat II except that he was succeeded by Senusret II around 1897 BCE. Senusret II had an extremely good relationship with the nomarchs. He was succeeded by Senusret III, who would lead Egypt into one of its golden ages.

Senusret III

Egyptian kings were usually associated with the gods, but some kings were so great that they were actively worshiped as gods. Senusret III was such a king. Not only was he worshiped as a god in Egypt and had his own cult that was on the same level as the great gods of the Egyptian pantheon, but he was also worshiped in Nubia. He was the son of Senusret II and had a privileged upbringing that included a royal education in Thebes. Senusret III took the throne around 1878 BCE. One of his first acts was to reorganize the government, thereby reducing the number of nomarchs. Strangely, there seems to have been little resistance to this reorganization. It's possible that Senusret III gave the disenfranchised nomarchs positions within his government.

Once his position was secure, he looked toward expanding Egypt's borders and came into conflict with Nubia, Syria, and Palestine. Senusret III was an extremely capable military leader, and many of his expeditions ended in success. In the past, nomarchs had standing armies that the king could call upon for aid, but Senusret absorbed those armies into his own large force. His actions also led to the development of the middle class in Egypt. During his reign, art became more elaborate and realistic. Some of the most famous pieces of art from his reign were his statues, which depicted the king during different times in his life.

Senusret III worked with the cult of Amun, which had historically struggled with the monarchy for power. This peaceful relationship benefited Egypt greatly. Few kings would ever live up to his enduring legacy. Senusret III died around 1839 BCE and was succeeded by his son, Amenemhet III.

Amenemhet III

Amenemhet III had the unenviable task of living up to the example of his father, who was the ideal Egyptian king. Amenemhet didn't leave behind many records of his military victories, which means that he probably didn't go to war as much as his father. He more than likely inherited a peaceful kingdom and didn't feel the need to defend his kingdom. It is also possible that he didn't feel the same need to expand Egypt's borders as his father did. Amenemhet did seem to enjoy initiating building projects, which led to the construction of many important monuments. Herodotus accredited Amenemhet III with building the legendary mortuary temple known as the Labyrinth. The ancient Greek historian claimed that Amenemhet III's mortuary temple at Hawara was one of the most impressive monuments in the ancient world.

Perhaps Amenemhet III's greatest achievement was creating a system that regulated the flow of water into Lake Moeris by draining the marshes surrounding the lake. He increased work at the turquoise mines located in Sinai and used quarries throughout Nubia and Egypt that provided necessary funds for his various building projects. Amenemhet III may not have had the same stellar reign as his father, but he was a capable king who increased Egypt's prosperity in his own right. He was succeeded by Amenemhat IV around 1815 BCE.

Sobekneferu

Amenemhat IV continued many of his father's policies and launched many of his own initiatives, which included building projects and military campaigns. Unfortunately, he seems to have had a short reign and died without a male heir. This would have been disastrous, as the previous kings seem to have appointed co-regents during their lifetime, which ensured a smooth transition of power. Since Amenemhet IV had no viable heir, there was no co-regent, and the transfer of power wouldn't have been easy. When Amenemhet IV died, the throne went to his wife or sister (or possibly both), Sobekneferu, around 1807 BCE. Not much is known about her reign except that she likely wasn't the first Egyptian queen to rule in her own right. An earlier queen, Nitiqret, is thought to have ruled for a short period during the Old Kingdom, but few records exist from her time.

Statue of Queen Sobekneferu.
https://commons.wikimedia.org/wiki/File:Statue_of_Sobekneferu_(Berlin_Egyptian_Muse um_14475).jpg

Whether or not Sobekneferu was the first queen of her kind, her reign was certainly remarkable. She reigned several hundred years before Hatshepsut, and she always ruled as a woman and never depicted herself as a man. She commissioned several important building projects, such as the city of Crocodilopolis, which she either founded or repaired. Unfortunately, she wasn't able to provide an heir and died around 1802 BCE, which effectively ended the Twelfth Dynasty.

The Decline of the Middle Kingdom

When Queen Sobekneferu died, the throne passed to Sobekhotep I, who began the Thirteenth Dynasty. While the Thirteenth Dynasty inherited a prosperous and strong country, the kings of this dynasty didn't seem to have the same drive and power as the kings of the Twelfth. Records during this time are rare and fragmented, which means it's difficult to know exactly what led to the decline of the Middle Kingdom. It seems the Thirteenth Dynasty kings were somewhat weaker than those of the Twelfth. While they kept many of the same policies, factions began to develop within Egypt. In time, Hyksos rose to become a powerful political power that rivaled the power of Iti-tawi.

As the Thirteenth Dynasty declined in power, the Hyksos came to rule Egypt. They showed great respect for the Egyptian culture and ruled during the Second Intermediate Period. In the past, the Second Intermediate Period had been characterized as a lawless time, but it seems that most people in Egypt enjoyed relative stability. The change in power would only have impacted Egypt's social elite.

There is no denying that the Middle Kingdom was a time of great prosperity for Egypt, and the achievements of the Twelfth Dynasty elevated Egypt to one of the most powerful and wealthy states in the world. Unfortunately, their successors were unable to keep up that prestige and buckled under the weight of their impressive empire, which led to the rise of a different power in the region.

While the Second Intermediate Period likely wasn't a time of complete chaos, it certainly was a far cry from the heights achieved by the Middle Kingdom. However, the Second Intermediate Period would lead to the New Kingdom and even greater heights for ancient Egypt.

Chapter 3: The New Kingdom (1550–1070 BCE)

Ancient Egypt enjoyed many golden periods during which great pyramids were built and elaborate art was developed. When the Middle Kingdom declined, a foreign influence, the Hyksos, managed to accrue wealth and political power that allowed them to take control of a significant portion of Egypt. In time, the Egyptian monarchy regained strength and drove the Hyksos out of Egypt. Once they were rid of the foreign power, the Egyptians set up boundaries that were supposed to prevent invasions but became stepping stones that helped future kings turn Egypt into a mighty empire.

The most prosperous Egyptian kingdom was the New Kingdom. During this era, literature, architecture, and trade flourished. Egypt became an international power, as it traded and corresponded with the major world powers of the time. More people were writing than ever before, which makes the New Kingdom one of the best-documented eras in ancient Egyptian history. This wealth of information has given modern people a clear look into one of the most fascinating periods in Egyptian history. The New Kingdom introduced legendary figures like Akhenaten, Hatshepsut,

Tutankhamun, and Ramesses II. It would also be the period during which Egyptian kings became known as pharaohs.

Hyksos

The Middle Kingdom was a time of incredible unity and prosperity for Egypt, during which the monarchy had firm control of Egypt. However, that power declined under the Thirteenth Dynasty kings, who couldn't live up to the example left by their predecessors. The kings of the Thirteenth Dynasty struggled to keep Egypt unified, and as a result, the Hyksos settled in Avaris, which was located in Lower Egypt. The Kingdom of Kush also gained power close to Upper Egypt, which presented another problem.

While the Hyksos were foreign, their rule wasn't completely unpopular. Later records would paint the Second Intermediate Period as a time of utter chaos, but this could have been a result of propaganda meant to highlight the rule of the New Kingdom kings against the rule of the Hyksos. The foreign rulers seemed to have had a relatively peaceful relationship with the rulers of Egypt and had a definite impact on Egyptian history. For example, the Hyksos influenced Egyptian warfare by introducing chariots and horses. They also brought bronze to Egypt, which allowed for stronger weapons and armor. The Hyksos may have originated from the north, which drew Egypt's attention to the Middle East and inspired future Egyptian kings to expand their empire northward.

Relations between the Hyksos and the Egyptian monarchy soured during the reign of King Seqenenra Taa of Egypt. He went to war against the Hyksos but was killed in battle. His son, Kamose of Thebes, continued his father's war and defeated the Hyksos, but it was Ahmose I who drove the Hyksos out of the kingdom and reunified Egypt.

Ahmose I

Ahmose I took the throne around 1550 BCE during a tumultuous time. He faced incredible odds yet managed to bring peace and stability to Egypt. The Hyksos were infamous for exacting tribute from the Egyptian kings and marrying Egyptian princesses, which may have indicated their intent to join themselves to the Egyptian monarchy. Ahmose I used horses, chariots, and bronze weapons to destroy Avaris and drive the Hyksos to Palestine and later to Syria. Once the Hyksos were driven out of the country, Ahmose reestablished Thebes as the capital of his kingdom and conquered Nubia again. This allowed him to plunder vast amounts of gold from Nubia, which increased Egypt's wealth. Ahmose I realized he had to take firm steps to prevent the Hyksos or others from invading his borders. As a result, he built forts in previously neglected areas and established buffer zones around the borders to protect Egypt from invasion.

Both sides of a ceremonial ax that belonged to Ahmose I.
Color photograph: Heidi Kontkanen (cc-by-sa-2.0 per original uploaded photograph)Black and white photograph: Mariette, Auguste (1821-1881) (Public Domain), CC BY-SA 2.0 https://creativecommons.org/licenses/by-sa/2.0 via Wikimedia Commons; https://commons.wikimedia.org/wiki/File:Ceremonial_axe_of_Ahmose_I_(both_sides).jpg

The Egyptian people venerated Ahmose I like a god, which was an honor that was only reserved for legendary kings. In an effort to boost the Egyptian economy, Ahmose reopened several mines, generating more trade for the country. His efforts established the New Kingdom, which would last for almost five centuries and bring increasing prosperity and fame to the empire. Ahmose I also fought against the Kushites and prevented them from invading Egypt, which was something his predecessors hadn't been able to do. For the first time in centuries, Egypt was united, and the central government was stable again. Ahmose I left a secure kingdom for his son, Amenhotep I, and was venerated along with Narmer as one of Egypt's great unifiers.

Hatshepsut

Amenhotep I was a competent king who made great contributions to art and left a stable throne for his son, Thutmose I, around 1520 BCE. Thutmose I was a warrior like his grandfather, Ahmose I. He expanded Egypt's hold on Nubia and set his sights on more territory and building projects. When he died, his designated heir was apparently his legitimate daughter, Hatshepsut (according to her inscriptions), but the throne went to his son, Thutmose II, who was born by a lesser queen. The siblings were married, as was the tradition at the time. Hatshepsut was the real power behind the throne and became one of the most influential kings of the New Kingdom. For the first seven years, she was depicted as a woman, but she later chose to be depicted as a male ruler.

Statue of Queen Hatshepsut.

Her reign brought great prosperity and stability to Egypt. She was appointed as the wife of the god Amun, which was an influential and powerful role in Egypt. In time, Thutmose II died, leaving behind his son by a lesser wife, Thutmose III. Hatshepsut retained her power and ruled as regent. Around the same time that she began presenting herself as a man, she also declared herself pharaoh. Like her predecessors, she initiated military campaigns and building projects. She also built a temple at Deir el-Bahari, which is one of the most impressive in all of Egypt, and made a lavish campaign to Punt. Hatshepsut commissioned more building projects than any other Egyptian monarch besides Ramesses the Great.

All throughout Hatshepsut's reign, Thutmose III proved his worth by acting as one of her generals. Around 1457 BCE, Thutmose III was sent to subdue a rebellion in Kadesh, and it was around that time Hatshepsut disappeared from history. It's possible that she died from an abscess in her tooth. Whatever the true cause of her death was, Thutmose III was made king and quickly began destroying records of his stepmother's reign. Her accomplishments were erased, and she remained a mystery until historians discovered evidence of her existence in the 19th century CE.

Thutmose III

It is unclear why Thutmose III decided to erase his stepmother's name from history, but a few theories prevail. Some historians think that Thutmose III wanted to restore the balance of Egyptian rulership since Egypt was usually ruled by males, while some think that Thutmose III wanted to prevent women from becoming too ambitious. Thanks to his stepmother's efforts, Thutmose III inherited a stable kingdom, which allowed him to set his sights on expanding Egypt's borders. In fact, Thutmose III was responsible for numerous successful military campaigns that stretched Egypt's borders farther than ever before.

Thutmose completed seventeen military campaigns in two decades and left ample inscriptions detailing his victories. He left so many inscriptions behind that he is one of the most well-known pharaohs in Egypt. When he died, he left the throne to his son Amenhotep II around 1425 BCE. Amenhotep wasn't as eager to go to war as his father and proved to be a capable ruler. He forged a peace treaty with the Mitanni and others. He left the throne to his son, Thutmose IV, around 1400 BCE. Thutmose imitated his father in many ways and restored the Great Sphinx.

Amenhotep III

Amenhotep III ascended to the throne when he was only twelve years old, but he had inherited one of the wealthiest kingdoms in the world. As soon as he was crowned, he married Tiye and elevated her to the rank of "Great Royal Wife," which meant she outranked every other female at court. He proved to be a capable diplomat who used his great wealth to foster good relationships with surrounding nations, usually buying their favor or paying them to do whatever he wanted. Amenhotep III was a good military leader, and some of his inscriptions detail his military campaigns, including a campaign to Nubia. However, his greatest interests lay in art, architecture, and religion.

Statue of Amenhotep III.

He commissioned over 250 building projects during his lifetime, most of which were massive and elaborate. Amenhotep III also granted his wife extraordinary powers, allowing her to govern the state while he was preoccupied. The two were often depicted together in carvings or statues. However, while the king continued to grow in wealth, so did the cult of Amun. When Amenhotep III took the throne, the priests of Amun owned as much land as the pharaoh. He saw the danger in this and allied himself with the god Aten, but this did little to curb the priests' power. His son, Amenhotep IV (later known as Akhenaten), would take more drastic measures. Amenhotep III died around 1353 BCE after an extremely successful reign.

Akhenaten

Akhenaten's reign began peacefully enough. He imitated many of his father's policies, but after a few years, he underwent a religious conversion and forced Egypt to go through several reforms. He made the ancient religion illegal and made Aten Egypt's principal deity. Akhenaten moved the capital to his new city, Akhetaten, and claimed that Aten was the supreme ruler of the universe. The king was the human embodiment of Aten. It's possible that his efforts reflected a sincere devotion to this god, but it's also possible that he wanted to reduce the cult of Amun's power. His reforms forced the cult to give up its vast wealth, but the changes also caused serious consequences for the country as a whole.

Akhenaten neglected foreign and state affairs, which resulted in the loss of vassal states and a general breakdown in the local government. His wife, Nefertiti, took over many of his duties and tried to rule the country in his stead as he became increasingly obsessed with his religion. Queen Nefertiti was a capable queen, but the country suffered from the king's neglect. Her power only went so far, and the royal treasury quickly became depleted. The religious reforms resulted in the loss of income for many artisans, which affected the economy. In addition, foreign affairs worsened as his reign continued. Akhenaten died in 1336 BCE, having undone much of his predecessors' efforts.

Tutankhamun

A few years later, Akhenaten's young son, Tutankhamun, took the throne. The eight-year-old king (some sources say nine-year-old king) tried his best to undo the damage done by his father and quickly reversed the religious reforms, restoring the ancient religion. He reopened temples and helped return some of Egypt's former glory. The ordinary people had suffered during the reformation, and Tutankhamun brought stability back to their lives. He married his wife and half-sister, Ankhesenamun, sometime during his reign but died before he could father any heirs. It is believed he died around 1327 BCE.

Statue of Tutankhamun.
EditorfromMars, CC BY-SA 4.0 https://creativecommons.org/licenses/by-sa/4.0 via Wikimedia Commons; https://commons.wikimedia.org/wiki/File:Tutankhamun,_Cairo_Museum.jpg

Ankhesenamun may have tried to take the throne for herself and famously wrote to King Suppiluliuma I of the Hittites to ask for one of his sons in marriage. The Hittite king sent his son to marry the Egyptian queen, but the prince disappeared during the journey. Tutankhamun's vizier, Ay, became the next pharaoh. Ay continued Tutankhamun's efforts to restore Egypt back to its former glory, but it was Ay's successor, Horemheb, who succeeded in completely reversing the religious reforms initiated by Akhenaten. Horemheb also died without an heir, leaving the throne to his vizier, Paramesse, who became Pharaoh Ramesses I around 1292 BCE.

Ramesses I

Ramesses was the first king of the Nineteenth Dynasty and was likely a close friend of Horemheb. Historians have theorized that Ramesses was part of a military family, which was how he became acquainted with Horemheb. Since Horemheb had no heirs, he appointed Ramesses as his heir, even though Ramesses was advanced in age by the time Horemheb died. It's possible that Horemheb appointed Ramesses since he had an heir. Ramesses took the throne around 1292 BCE and appointed his son, Seti I, as his co-regent. It's likely that Ramesses found it difficult to keep up with his kingly responsibilities or wanted his son to learn how to be a capable king.

Seti I immediately began military campaigns and aimed to regain Egypt's former lands in Syria. In the meantime, Ramesses I busied himself with numerous building projects in Egypt. Ramesses I died after a short reign, which lasted fewer than two years, and left the throne to Seti I. Like his predecessors, Seti poured much of his energy into returning Egypt to its former glory. Seti I commissioned various building projects and began teaching his son how to be a good king. He proved to be a capable ruler. While he did his best to return to the prosperity Egypt had enjoyed under Amenhotep III, it would be his son, Ramesses II, who would become one of the greatest pharaohs in Egyptian history.

Ramesses II

Ramesses II took the throne around 1279 BCE and lived to be almost a hundred years old. When he died, many of his subjects could not remember living under a different ruler, which caused the people to panic. From a young age, Ramesses joined his father on military campaigns and soon began leading his own military expeditions. He fought against the Hittites and secured Egypt's borders while expanding trade routes. Ramesses defeated the Sea Peoples, who were allied with the Hittites, and incorporated them into his own army. He also built the city of Per-Ramesses, which is said to have rivaled the ancient city of Thebes.

In 1274, he fought in the Battle of Kadesh, which ended in a draw. However, the king claimed to have won the battle to boost his own reputation. Later, he was part of the world's first peace treaty when he negotiated with the Hittites. He was also a great patron of the arts, and many historians claim that ancient Egyptian art reached its peak during his rule. Ramesses II commissioned many building projects and left behind a large number of inscriptions. He also had the Tomb of Nefertari built. Nefertari was his favorite wife who died early in his reign, and her tomb was magnificently constructed to reflect the king's favor. Ramesses had Nefertari's likeness carved alongside him in many of his carvings long after she died, which shows the depth of his devotion to his first wife.

Temple of Ramesses II at Abu Simbel.
Merlin UK, CC BY-SA 3.0 https://creativecommons.org/licenses/by-sa/3.0 via Wikimedia Commons; https://commons.wikimedia.org/wiki/File:Temple_of_Ramese_II_at_Abu_Simbel_-_panoramio.jpg

During Ramesses II's reign, he strengthened the borders, increased trade, and replenished Egypt's coffers. His achievements made him one of the greatest pharaohs in history, and he was deeply loved and revered by the ancient Egyptians. He was succeeded by his heir, Merneptah, around 1213 BCE, who was already an old man when he became king. Merneptah was eager to prove himself and launched various successful military campaigns.

He was succeeded for a short period by Amenmesse around 1203 BCE, who may have been a usurper since the rightful heir was supposed to be Seti II. Around 1200 BCE, Amenmesse was no longer mentioned in the records. Seti II reigned to about 1197 BCE and was succeeded by Merneptah Siptah, who inherited the throne as a boy and died young. His stepmother, Tausret, ruled as regent until 1190 BCE until she was succeeded by Setnakht, who was likely another usurper.

Ramesses III

Setnakht may have been one of Seti II's sons. He established the Twentieth Dynasty. He was succeeded by Ramesses III, who proved to be a capable king and the last great king of the New Kingdom. He began his reign by driving off the Sea Peoples and strengthening the country's government. During his reign, the Libyans tried to invade the country, but Ramesses III defeated them in battle and secured Egypt's borders, proving his capabilities as a warrior king. He also built his great mortuary temple in between intermittent fighting against would-be invaders. Trade and industry flourished under his reign, and he used many of Egypt's mines to boost the economy.

However, Ramesses III's reign wasn't completely successful, as he experienced one of the first labor strikes in history. Workers on one of his building projects were unsatisfied with working conditions and refused to work until the problems were fixed. Ramesses III faced serious political instability during his reign and was assassinated around 1155 BCE.

The Decline of the New Kingdom

Akhenaten may have brought his country to the edge of decline during his rule in an attempt to curb the power of the priests of Amun. When his religious reforms were reversed, the cult of Amun was restored, and it continued to amass power and wealth at the expense of the crown. By the time Ramesses III took the throne, the pharaoh's power was nowhere near what it had been during the time of Amenhotep III. Ramesses III was succeeded by his son Ramesses IV, with many of his successors also named Ramesses. However, they shared no similarities with Ramesses the Great, as the monarchy declined rapidly during the reign of the Twentieth Dynasty's kings.

The priests of Amun were left unchecked. This allowed them to effectively divide Egypt into two and take power away from the monarchy until the central government was crippled. Ramesses I had left Thebes centuries prior, which allowed the priests to take control of the ancient city and extend their influence. In time, the king came to represent a subordinate of Amun, which, by extension, made him a subordinate of the priests. Soon, the Nubians took much of southern Egypt while the priests governed Upper Egypt, which led to the Third Intermediate Period. Unfortunately, there wouldn't be another great kingdom to drag Egypt out of the chaos. The Third Intermediate Period ended with the Battle of Pelusium in 525 BCE, which led to the Persian invasion.

Chapter 4: The End of Ancient Egypt (1070–330 BCE)

The Third Intermediate Period brought an end to the glory of ancient Egypt. The New Kingdom was defined by remarkable rulers who fostered diplomatic relationships and expanded Egypt's borders while ensuring that Egypt was stable. They brought immense prosperity to Egypt and built magnificent monuments that still attract tourists today. Unfortunately, by the time the New Kingdom's last great pharaoh took the throne, Egypt was a shadow of its former self and riddled with problems due to religious reforms and issues with succession.

When the Twentieth Dynasty came to an end, so did the New Kingdom. During the Third Intermediate Period, the pharaohs would become almost inconsequential as the cult of Amun seized power in Egypt. As time wore on, Egypt became a battleground for Nubia and Assyria as those foreign powers battled for Egypt's wealth. Before long, the Persians invaded Egypt and would rule over the region for several decades before Alexander the Great arrived and claimed the country as his own. While Egypt remained a strong and influential region, the glittering age of pharaohs and pyramids was over.

The Decline of the Pharaohs

For decades, the cult of Amun's power had grown at the expense of the monarchy. While the pharaohs of the New Kingdom usually managed to keep the cult of Amun in check, the pharaohs of the Twentieth Dynasty were unable to do so, which would have lasting consequences for Egypt as a whole. The Twentieth Dynasty ended with the reign of Pharaoh Ramesses XI, who died around 1077 BCE. For much of Egypt's history, the pharaohs were seen as extensions of the deities, living gods who enacted the will of the gods on Earth. This status made them all-powerful, and their authority was completely accepted by their subjects. The ancient Egyptians were influenced by their religion and did not dare question the will of the gods.

However, as time went on, pharaohs became known as the children of deities, which curbed their power. The priests became the intermediaries between humans and the gods. This placed incredible power in the hands of the priests, who lived at the temples and claimed vast amounts of land and wealth on behalf of the gods. When Ramesses XI died, he was succeeded by Smendes, a government official from Lower Egypt who started the Twenty-first Dynasty. Smendes moved from Per-Ramesses to Tanis, while the cult of Amun ruled from Thebes. Once again, Egypt was divided, but there is no evidence that this separation was caused by a civil war. It would appear as though the monarchy took care of the administrative duties from Tanis, while the priests ruled in Amun's name from Thebes. This would have required remarkable cooperation, and it doesn't seem as though the two parties were enemies.

Cult of Amun

For much of Egypt's history, Thebes was considered the home of the god Amun. During the New Kingdom, Amun became the most important deity in the Egyptian pantheon and had a similar role in Egyptian culture as Zeus had in Greek culture. Sometime during the rule of Ahmose I, Amun was fused with the sun god Ra and became Amun-Ra. As Thebes rose in importance, so did Amun, which may also explain why the god became so important to the Egyptians. His temple was located at the Karnak temple complex, which was built near Luxor. Its construction began during Senusret I's rule, and it became a custom of the pharaohs to add to it during their reign. This allowed Karnak to become the largest religious building in the world and brought great pride to the Egyptians.

Temple Complex at Karnak
Cornell University Library, CC BY 2.0 https://creativecommons.org/licenses/by/2.0, via Wikimedia Commons; https://commons.wikimedia.org/wiki/File:Temple_Complex_at_Karnak.jpg

Since Amun became such an important god, his cult also grew in importance. The priests, especially the high priests, were thought to have a direct link to the god, which made them extremely important since they would have had contact with every sort of Egyptian citizen. By the end of the New Kingdom, there were as many as eighty thousand priests who lived and worked at Karnak. The cult of Amun also owned more land and wealth than the pharaoh, which had a definite impact on the monarch's influence. During the Third Intermediate Period, Amun was effectively the king of Thebes. The priests used oracles to determine the god's will to solve judicial, domestic, and political issues. By the Third Intermediate Period,

Thebes had become a complete theocracy, and the priests regularly communicated with Amun as if he was the pharaoh. The kings in Tanis would oversee what the elusive god couldn't.

Nubian Conquest

During the Middle and New Kingdoms, Egyptian pharaohs pushed their way into Nubia and either conquered or exacted tribute from the Nubians. Nubia and Egypt had close ties for most of their history since they both relied on the Nile. When the Egyptian pharaohs conquered Nubia during the Middle and New Kingdom periods, they carried over their god Amun. During these times, the Egyptians built numerous temples to Amun and declared that Nubia was Amun's southern residence. This promoted the worship of Amun and legitimized the Egyptians' claim to Nubia. The Egyptians were interested in Nubia because it was abundant in natural resources, such as ivory, ebony, animal skins, and gold.

The close relationship between the two countries led to cultural and religious ties that would endure for centuries. However, as Egypt began declining in power, Nubia used the basis laid by former Egyptian pharaohs as an excuse to invade Egypt. In the 700s BCE, the Kushite king, Piye, was able to annex Karnak and went on to conquer the rest of Egypt. He claimed to be working on behalf of Amun, and he became the first Kushite pharaoh in 744 BCE. Since the Nubians already worshiped Amun, his cult was allowed to continue its duties and enjoyed significant influence over both Egypt and Nubia. When Piye ruled Egypt, he allowed the kings of Lower Egypt to have a measure of power. The Kushite kings had immense respect for the Egyptian culture, and their rule didn't have a negative impact on Egyptian culture as a whole.

Assyria vs. Egypt

For much of Egypt's history, Egyptian kings had purposefully created buffer zones along their borders, which prevented the borders from clashing with powerful enemies who could potentially invade Egypt. However, during the Third Intermediate Period, many of these buffer zones were defeated. They were added to Egypt's territory but also left the state vulnerable to foreign invasion. Around 926 BCE, Pharaoh Shoshenq I conquered Judah. This was considered to be a massive victory, but it also brought Egypt into contact with the Assyrians. When the Kushite king, Piye, died, he was succeeded by his brother, Shabaka. Later, Shebitku, Shabaka's successor, lent support to Judah against the Assyrian king, Sennacherib. This would have been enough to draw Assyria's hostility.

In 671 BCE, Egypt was ruled by Taharqa when the Assyrian king, Esarhaddon, marched against Egypt. He invaded the country and took the royal family hostage. Taharqa was able to escape to Egypt and was succeeded by Tantamani. Tantamani was able to temporarily overthrow Assyrian rule, but he was quickly conquered by Esarhaddon's son, Ashurbanipal, in 666 BCE, who left a puppet king, Necho I, on the throne of Egypt.

Sack of Thebes

While the Kushites maintained a strong hold on Egypt, their influence gradually declined during the Twenty-fifth Dynasty. Tantamani, for the most part, had control of Upper Egypt and Nubia. He still held Thebes, which was an incredibly important foothold. However, in 663 BCE, Ashurbanipal and Tantamani were locked in a war that would determine the outcome of Egypt's future. For a brief period, Tantamani gained the upper hand and was able to conquer Memphis, where he killed the puppet king, Necho I. As a result, Ashurbanipal and Psamtik (Necho I's son) met the Kushite king in battle near Memphis. The Kushites were defeated, and Tantamani retreated to Nubia, which left the ancient city of Thebes unprotected.

Thebes fell to the Assyrian forces and was thoroughly sacked. Most of its riches and inhabitants were carried off to Assyria. It was a resounding catastrophe that left a definite mark on Egyptian history and morale. The sack of Thebes brought a decisive end to the Twenty-fifth Dynasty, as the Kushite kings were never able to regain the land that they had lost. Thebes had been so thoroughly defeated that, six years later, it surrendered to Psamtik's fleet.

Psamtik became king of Egypt and founded the Twenty-sixth Dynasty, which brought an end to the Third Intermediate Period and began the Late Period. The king had Thebes accept his daughter, Nitocris I, as the God's Wife of Amun, which was an incredibly important position in Egypt.

Psamtik was a capable leader who brought peace and unity to Egypt. He commissioned many monuments, restored old buildings, and was a strong military leader. He was succeeded by Necho II, who created an Egyptian navy made up of Greek mercenaries. Necho II was succeeded by Psamtik II around 595 BCE, who proved himself in battle against Kush and famously erased the names of Kushite kings from southern monuments, even going as far as to try and erase his father's name from history. The reasons for his actions are still unknown. He was succeeded by his son, Apries, around 589 BCE. Apries was overthrown in a coup orchestrated by his father's general, Amasis II.

Amasis II

Apries proved to be an unsuccessful military leader. He tried to fight the Babylonians but lost. When he lost his throne, he appealed to the Babylonians for help and was probably killed on the battlefield when he faced Amasis II's army. It is possible that Amasis II was responsible for Psamtik II's victories in Nubia. Psamtik II never did much with his military victories, instead choosing to return to Egypt without firmly establishing his rule. That must have frustrated Amasis II and may have led to his coup.

Amasis II was the strongest pharaoh in centuries and helped return Egypt to some of its former glory. He stimulated the economy and conducted several successful military campaigns. Under his rule, building projects abounded, the economy flourished, and the borders were secure. The art industry received a tremendous boost, which only added to Amasis II's reputation.

While Amasis II was a capable king, he failed Egypt in two fundamental ways. His son, Psamtik III, was wholly unprepared for the challenges of ruling Egypt when he ascended to the throne around 526 BCE. Amasis II may have also been responsible for the Persian invasion. According to the Greek historian Herodotus, the Persian king, Cambyses II, requested to marry one of Amasis's daughters. The Egyptians famously refused to give any of their noblewomen to foreigners, and Amasis wanted to uphold that tradition without making a deadly enemy. In response, he sent one of Apries's daughters to marry Cambyses II. The former princess was so offended by Amasis's actions that she revealed her identity to Cambyses II as soon as she arrived at her destination. This enraged Cambyses II, and according to tradition, he swore revenge on the Egyptians.

Bastet and the Divine Cats

Animals were usually sacred to the Egyptians since they represented various aspects of gods in the Egyptian pantheon. People usually mummified their pets when they died and took great care of them during their life. While most animals were highly regarded, cats were sacred in Egypt. They were the most common pets, and their popularity was directly linked to Bastet.

Statue of the goddess Bastet.
Rama, CC BY-SA 3.0 FR https://creativecommons.org/licenses/by-sa/3.0/fr/deed.en , via Wikimedia Commons; https://commons.wikimedia.org/wiki/File:Bastet-E_3731-IMG_0549-gradient.jpg

The goddess Bastet was immensely popular, and the Egyptians were terrified of offending her. Bastet was the goddess of women's secrets, fertility, cats, childbirth, and the home. She protected houses, women, and children from disease and harmful spirits. Her role also extended to the afterlife, and she was known for being extremely vengeful. At first, she was associated with the goddess Sekhmet, the goddess of war who destroyed Ra's enemies, since she had inherited some of Sekhmet's more terrifying qualities. Bastet became so influential that people believed she helped correct injustices.

The Egyptians believed that if Bastet was offended, she would unleash devastating plagues on humanity. One way to offend the goddess was by killing a cat. The punishment for killing a cat in ancient Egypt was death. According to Herodotus, if a building was on fire, the cats had to be saved first. And if a household's cat died, they had to shave their eyebrows as a sign of respect to avoid the goddess's wrath.

The Battle of Pelusium

When Cambyses II decided to invade Egypt in 525 BCE, it became clear that he needed to defeat the city of Pelusium to gain access to the rest of the country. The only problem was that Pelusium was highly fortified and would likely only fall after a lengthy battle. Cambyses II was undeterred and mobilized his forces against the city but was quickly driven back. The king was determined to conquer Egypt and came up with a creative plan. The Egyptians' respect and love for cats were well established. As a result, Cambyses had his forces capture various stray animals, mostly cats. His army was then commanded to paint the image of Bastet on their shields. When his army advanced on Pelusium a second time, they drove the animals ahead of them.

As a result, the Egyptians were forced to surrender or risk offending Bastet, which they believed would bring great disaster down upon them. Pelusium fell, and Cambyses II marched through the streets in victory. According to legend, Cambyses threw cats at the Egyptians during this march in order to taunt them. From there, Cambyses II conquered the rest of Egypt.

Persian Rule

It's unlikely that Cambyses II invaded Egypt because of a perceived insult, but Amasis II's actions may have provided him with the excuse he needed to go to war. The Assyrians had proven that the Egyptians weren't equipped to win a war against foreign armies, and the Persians were becoming increasingly powerful and eager to expand their territory. Egypt's riches and cultures were well known in the ancient world, so the nation would have been an irresistible temptation to the Persian king.

Unfortunately for Egypt, Psamtik III was unprepared for the invading Persian forces, and Egypt quickly fell to the Persian army. When Egypt was defeated, Cambyses II took the Egyptian royal family and many nobles to his capital at Susa. Apparently, many nobles and much of the royal family were executed. Psamtik was allowed to live at the Persian court. He was executed shortly after when it was discovered that he was planning a revolt against the Persians. When Psamtik III died, the Third Intermediate Period and the Twenty-sixth Dynasty ended with him.

Accounts vary about Persian rule over Egypt. The Greeks claimed that Cambyses was a tyrannical despot who burned Egyptian temples and showed no respect for the Egyptian culture. However, an Egyptian admiral, Wedjahor-Resne, who was a contemporary of Cambyses II, claimed that the Persian king greatly respected the Egyptians and endeavored to show respect for his new subjects' culture. Unfortunately for the Egyptians, many of them were enslaved by the Persians and forced to serve in Cambyses's army. The Persians managed to maintain a relatively firm hold of Egypt until 331 BCE, when Alexander the Great arrived.

Alexander the Great in Egypt

Alexander the Great was one of the most accomplished military leaders in the world. He conquered many territories and expanded Greek influence farther than it had ever gone before. When he conquered Tyre, he set his sights on Egypt. Many of the towns on the way from Tyre to Egypt quickly submitted to his rule rather than face utter destruction. Unfortunately, Alexander faced trouble in Gaza. The fort was well protected and located on a large hill, which required Alexander to undertake a siege. He was forced to retreat a few times, but his famous determination pushed him to keep fighting until Gaza fell. When the fortress was finally defeated, the women and children became slaves, while the men were executed.

Alexander founding Alexandria
https://commons.wikimedia.org/wiki/File:Alexander_the_Great_Founding_Alexandria.jpg

From there, he advanced farther into Egypt and took large portions of territory away from the Persians. The Egyptians eagerly welcomed Alexander into their midst and quickly crowned him king at Memphis since they were desperate to be rid of the Persians. During the Persian rule, many Egyptian temples had been neglected. Alexander won favor with the Egyptians by renovating temples, building monuments, reforming the taxation system, and organizing his military.

In 332 BCE, Alexander sought to legitimize his rule by making large sacrifices to the Egyptian gods and honoring the oracle of Amun-Ra. The Egyptians proclaimed him the son of Amun, and he responded by calling Zeus-Amun his true father. His image was stamped on coins and showed him wearing the horns of Amun, which were meant to symbolize his right to rule. He went on to build the famous city of Alexandria and left a lasting mark on Egyptian history. When he died, he was succeeded by Ptolemy I, who founded the Ptolemaic dynasty.

PART TWO: An Overview of Modern Egypt (332 BCE–2021 CE)

Chapter 5: The Greco-Roman Period (332 BCE–629 CE)

The Greco-Roman period spanned from the time Alexander the Great left Egypt and lasted until the Rashidun conquest of Egypt around 639 CE. This period was marked by great advances in philosophy and science, as well as the Greek and Roman rulers who reigned over Egypt during those years. The culture and religion that marked Egypt's ancient era would mix and form close ties with the Greek and Roman cultures. During this period, Egypt's famous Ptolemaic dynasty rose to power. The Ptolemies were a Macedonian family that ruled over Egypt for centuries while retaining their Greek identity. This was accomplished through intermarriages that kept the Ptolemies strictly Greek.

The last Ptolemaic pharaoh, Cleopatra VII, would form unbreakable ties with Rome and take part in a bloody Roman civil war. Unfortunately, Cleopatra's forces lost, and Egypt became a Roman province. Egypt would serve as Rome's breadbasket until Diocletian split the Roman Empire into two. Egypt became part of the Byzantine Empire. The Greco-Roman period was one of the most influential periods in Egyptian, Greek, and Roman history. During this time, empires rose and fell, Alexandria rose in prominence, and important monuments were built. Some of the most famous figures in history existed during this age and left their mark on history. Egypt left its ancient heritage firmly in the past as it influenced and interacted with the most powerful empires of its time.

Ptolemy I Soter

Ptolemy was a Macedonian nobleman who may have been Alexander the Great's half-brother through Alexander's father, Philip II. Officially, Ptolemy's father was another nobleman named Lagos, and although Ptolemy was older than Alexander, the two became close friends. Ptolemy acted as a historian and recorded many of Alexander's feats while noting his own involvement in various battles. He was also likely at Alexander's side in 332 BCE when Alexander was in Egypt. It was during this time that Ptolemy became one of Alexander's personal bodyguards. This is a clear indication of how highly Alexander esteemed Ptolemy.

Ptolemy I as an Egyptian pharaoh.
https://commons.wikimedia.org/wiki/File:Ring_with_engraved_portrait_of_Ptolemy_VI_P hilometor_(3rd%E2%80%932nd_century_BCE)_-_2009.jpg

When Alexander died in 323 BCE, he gave his signet ring to his cavalry leader, Perdiccas, which may have signified Alexander's intention to transfer power to him. Perdiccas decided to keep the empire intact since Alexander's wife, Roxana, was pregnant with a possible heir. However, Alexander's generals, led by Ptolemy, divided the empire amongst themselves, which led to the Wars of the Diadochi (or the Successor Wars). Perdiccas and Ptolemy hated each other, and this hatred culminated in a shocking event—the theft of Alexander the Great's body. Perdiccas sent Alexander's body to be interred in a tomb in Macedonia, but Ptolemy intercepted the body en route and had Alexander buried in a tomb in Alexandria. Perdiccas was disgusted and tried to attack Egypt but failed three times before his men became fed up with him and had him executed.

Ptolemy focused all his attention on ruling Egypt, unlike the other generals who tried to conquer as much territory as they could. He moved Egypt's capital to Alexandria to avoid the power of the priests and managed to stabilize the Egyptian economy. Under Ptolemy's guidance, Alexandria became a primarily Greek city. In order to legitimize his rule, he deified Alexander the Great and declared that he was Alexander's heir. He built a massive museum and library in Alexandria and also started construction on the Lighthouse of Alexandria. Ptolemy I died around 282 BCE and left behind the firmly established Ptolemaic dynasty, which would reign over Egypt for almost three centuries.

Alexandria

Alexandria is a port city on the coast of the Mediterranean Sea in Egypt, and it was founded by Alexander the Great around 331 BCE. The city quickly became popular after it was built and attracted thousands of inhabitants. Its influence grew after it became the capital of Egypt during the Ptolemaic dynasty. The city housed the famous Lighthouse of Alexandria, which became one of the Seven Wonders of the Ancient World. One could also find the

Library of Alexandria, which attracted some of the most prominent scholars in the world. Alexander intended Alexandria to connect Greece to Egypt. Although Alexander never returned to Alexandria once he left Egypt, the city accomplished its purpose and became a center of Hellenistic culture.

Lighthouse of Alexandria.
https://commons.wikimedia.org/wiki/File:Philip_Galle_-
_Lighthouse_of_Alexandria_(Pharos_of_Alexandria)_-_1572.jpg

Alexandria became home to Greeks, Egyptians, and Jews. The Septuagint, which was a Greek version of the Tanakh (the Hebrew Bible, which includes the Torah, Ketuvim, and Nevi'im), was produced in Alexandria. Ptolemy I had his own vision for Alexandria and wanted to turn it into a prominent and influential community in the Mediterranean. He built the Library of Alexandria and a museum and started construction on the Lighthouse of Alexandria. The library collected thousands of papyrus scrolls filled with knowledge about subjects like history, literature, science, and philosophy. Scholars from all over the ancient world, especially Greece, flocked to the library. The city reflected the glory of the Ptolemaic dynasty, and the ruling family hardly ever left the capital.

Hellenistic Influences on Egypt

It's unsurprising that Egypt was deeply influenced by the Greek language, religion, and culture since its ruling dynasty was proudly Greek. Ptolemy I chose Egypt as his inheritance from Alexander the Great since the country was rich in natural resources and was on good terms with the Greeks. Soon, Egypt was flooded by Greek residents. Ptolemy built a new city in Upper Egypt named Ptolemais to house all the new immigrants. The Ptolemaic dynasty showed great respect for the Egyptian culture but made few attempts to immerse themselves in Egyptian traditions. In fact, the famous Cleopatra VII, the last of the pharaohs, was the only Ptolemaic ruler who learned to speak Egyptian.

The Ptolemies were careful not to upset the established order in Egypt and basically left the Egyptian religion alone. The Egyptian priests were allowed to function as normal and even retained their elite social status. In order to endear themselves to the Egyptians, Ptolemy I returned many religious artifacts that had been stolen by the Persians. He also established the cult of Alexander the Great and the cult of Serapis, a healing god. Serapis's cult never gained popularity and eventually faded away. The Ptolemies introduced many Hellenistic aspects to Egyptian culture and made Greek the official language of the government and economy. For most of the Ptolemaic dynasty, these Egyptian and Greek influences coexisted in harmony.

The Ptolemaic Dynasty

Ptolemy II Philadelphus succeeded his father, Ptolemy I, to the throne around 282 BCE and married Arsinoe I, the daughter of the Thracian King Lysimachus. In return, Lysimachus married Ptolemy II's sister, Arsinoe II. When Lysimachus died, Ptolemy II married Arsinoe II. He fought the Syrian Wars from 260 to 252 BCE, built several trading posts, completed the Pharos (Lighthouse of

Alexandria), and established the Ptolemaieia festival. Ptolemy II was known as one of the great pharaohs of Egypt. Unfortunately, the Ptolemaic dynasty would be known for petty jealousy, betrayal, and incest, the latter being something they carried over from the previous Egyptian dynasties.

Ptolemy III succeeded his father around 246 BCE and married Berenice II. When one of their daughters, also named Berenice, died, the Canopus Decree was instituted, which made Berenice a goddess and suggested a new calendar that consisted of 365 days in a year with a leap year every 4 years. However, this calendar wasn't instituted. Ptolemy IV came to the throne around 221 BCE and married his sister, Arsinoe III. He gained some success in the Fourth Syrian War and built the Sema, which was meant to honor the Ptolemies and Alexander the Great. Ptolemy IV and Arsinoe III were the victims of a coup around 205 BCE.

Ptolemy V inherited the throne as a child but faced a series of wars that caused the loss of several Egyptian territories. Ptolemy VI also inherited the throne as a young child and ruled alongside his mother. Unfortunately, his reign was also beset with problems, as he fought outside invaders and his own brother, Ptolemy VIII. Ptolemy VI died in battle around 145 BCE and left the throne to Ptolemy VIII.

Ptolemy VIII was widely hated, and a civil war broke out that lasted from 132 to 124 BCE. Throughout the Ptolemaic dynasty, the royal family and the inhabitants of Alexandria experienced a tumultuous relationship, which led to several rebellions. Ptolemy VIII was succeeded by Ptolemy IX, who was overthrown by his brother for a brief period before he was able to regain the throne.

Meanwhile, Rome was beginning to rise as a formidable power. Several Ptolemaic pharaohs earned distrust from their citizens when they formed close relationships with Rome. Egypt realized that it was only a matter of time before Rome tried to conquer the rich country. The next few pharaohs had relatively little impact. Ptolemy

XIII became pharaoh in 51 BCE and married his sister, Cleopatra VII. Ptolemy XIII and his sister Arsinoe fought against Cleopatra and Julius Caesar and were defeated in battle. Arsinoe was taken as prisoner while Ptolemy XIII drowned in battle. Caesar replaced Ptolemy XIII with Ptolemy XIV, who ruled alongside Cleopatra until she allegedly had him poisoned.

Finally, Cleopatra VII took the throne in her own right, becoming the last Egyptian pharaoh.

The Battle of Actium

When Cleopatra took the Egyptian throne in 51 BCE, she began making friends with Rome and her own people. She had a great interest in Egyptian culture and even learned the language. However, when Julius Caesar died in 44 BCE, Rome was gripped by a civil war that ended with the Second Triumvirate, a coalition made up of Julius Caesar's heirs: Octavian, Mark Antony, and Lepidus. The Triumvirate split the empire into manageable portions. Mark Antony chose to rule the eastern part of the empire, which put him into direct contact with Cleopatra. The two began a tempestuous affair.

Battle of Actium
https://commons.wikimedia.org/wiki/File:Castro_Battle_of_Actium.jpg

The relationship between the Triumvirate deteriorated, and soon, Mark Antony and Octavian were locked in a heated feud that culminated in the Battle of Actium in 31 BCE. The two opposing forces used their fleets in the battle, and while Cleopatra supplied Mark Antony with abundant resources, he lost. Mark Antony and Cleopatra were able to escape with some of their ships. A year later, Octavian arrived in Egypt to claim his prize. Mark Antony was killed in battle, and Cleopatra committed suicide. Cleopatra's son by Caesar, Caesarion (the rightful heir to Egypt), was executed by Octavian, who became Caesar Augustus in 27 BCE. Egypt was assimilated into the Roman Empire.

Roman Egypt

During the height of the Roman Empire, the Mediterranean was referred to as the Roman Lake. Egypt became the empire's breadbasket. Crops and food were exported out of Egypt and transported to the rest of the Roman Empire. Egypt's resources were systematically plundered for the good of Rome. For the most part, Rome respected the Egyptian culture, and the Egyptians were allowed to continue as they had under the Ptolemaic dynasty. One of the biggest changes was the fact that Egypt was subject to Roman law, which had precedence over any Egyptian laws. Rome kept control of Egypt through an appointed governor. A flotilla was stationed on the Nile, and three legions ensured Roman control on land.

The Egyptian religion was allowed to remain, but Hellenic citizens received priority and soon made up the elite classes. Major cities had experienced the most influence from the Hellenistic culture, while Egyptian peasants and rural areas still conformed to the old traditions and culture. Under the Roman Empire, the aristocracy was allowed to gain land for themselves and quickly obtained control of massive private estates. Food, spices, and other luxury items from the East were transported along the Nile to Alexandria and then on to the rest of the empire. Soon, Alexandria had a massive Greek and Jewish population, which sometimes led to problems for the Roman emperors. For example, the Jewish population tried to burn down Alexandria's amphitheater during Nero's reign. About fifty thousand people died during the riot, and Rome dispatched two legions to deal with the problem.

At first, Egypt accepted Roman occupation, but by 115 CE, riots had broken out, and it became evident that the Egyptians were tired of Roman rule. For the next few decades, Egypt would continually be a place of riots and rebellions against the Romans until Rome eventually fell.

Vespasian

When Nero died around 68 CE, a series of civil wars broke out as the Romans tried to determine who would be their new leader. Four men tried to make their claim on the Roman throne, which led to the Year of the Four Emperors. Galba, Otho, Vespasian, and Vitellius each tried to become the next emperor of Rome. In time, Vitellius and Vespasian were the only contenders left.

A bust of Vespasian.
Imperator_Caesar_Vespasianus_Augustus_Vaux.jpg: Jebulonderivative work: Jebulon, CC0, via Wikimedia Commons;
https://commons.wikimedia.org/wiki/File:Imperator_Caesar_Vespasianus_Augustus_Vaux_1.jpg

Vespasian was from relatively humble origins; his father was a knight and former tax collector. In time, Vespasian joined the Roman Senate and enjoyed a successful military career that led to his praetorship in 39. He made sure to keep on the good side of the next few Roman emperors, including Claudius and Nero. During the power struggle to determine the next emperor of Rome, Vespasian refrained from the fighting since he didn't expect to win against Galba. However, when Galba was murdered, Vespasian emerged as a contender for the throne. Otho was defeated and committed suicide. Vespasian traveled to Alexandria in the hopes of sabotaging Vitellius's supply lines. During that time, Vespasian's allies managed to defeat Vitellius, who was killed in Rome. Vespasian was left as the clear winner and was declared the emperor of Rome while still in Alexandria.

As soon as Vespasian was emperor, he began looking for ways to stabilize the empire after the disastrous rule of Nero and the subsequent civil wars. He increased Rome's revenues (although his financial policies were immensely unpopular and caused discontent in Egypt) and stabilized the military. He died around 79 after a long and successful career.

Diocletian

By 284, the days of remarkable Roman emperors, such as Vespasian and Augustus, were long over. The Roman Empire was a shadow of its former self and faced serious rebellions and unrest. All that changed when Diocletian took the throne. Diocletian was born in the Balkan province around 245. He joined the military and quickly rose to prominence. He served under Emperor Carus as one of the emperor's imperial bodyguards. When Carus died, he left the throne to his son, Numerian, who was likely killed by his father-in-law, Arrius Aper. Diocletian avenged the emperor's death and became the Roman emperor in November 284.

Diocletian realized that Rome had become too large to rule effectively and split the empire in two. He appointed his son-in-law,

Maximian, as Caesar of the West Roman Empire while he oversaw the East. Diocletian managed to win great victories in the East against Persia and along the Danube River. He abdicated the throne along with Maximian in 305 and retired to his massive palace in modern-day Croatia. Unfortunately, the Roman Empire was plagued by more problems in the following decades. The Western Roman Empire fell in 476, while the Eastern Roman Empire continued. The Eastern half of the empire is also known as the Byzantine Empire.

The Byzantine Empire

Diocletian was the last Roman emperor who personally visited Egypt. When the Roman Empire was split into two parts, the West ceased having a major effect on Egypt. In 330, Constantinople was formed, which took away some of Alexandria's influence. However, Constantinople still needed grain from Egypt, and Egypt soon became a politically important part of the Eastern Roman Empire. In time, the Byzantine Empire turned into a Christian state. Greco-Roman influences faded as "Oriental" influences took over. However, Alexandria remained an influential city that was dominated by religious violence.

In the 5th century, Egypt was controlled by several important Christian churches. Christianity quickly gained popularity since it appealed to the rich and poor alike. Churches and monasteries provided communal buildings, such as water cisterns, bakeries, workshops, stables, kitchens, and other resources that allowed communities to become prosperous and self-sufficient. However, the churches were dominated by rival patriarchs who fought each other for power. The religion became complicated and political, which may have contributed to the downfall of Christianity during the Arab invasion in the 7th century. While Islam attracted many followers in the region, Christianity remained in Egypt for the next few centuries.

Philosophy in Egypt

For many centuries, the Greeks regarded Egypt as a place of philosophy and knowledge. Many Greek scholars and philosophers were attracted to Egypt, Alexandria in particular, when the Ptolemies took control of the country. According to legend, Pythagoras traveled to Egypt to gain more knowledge since the Egyptians were known for their philosophical pursuits. Pythagoras was accredited with bringing philosophy to the Greeks, at least according to the famous Greek scholar Isocrates. Plato believed the Egyptians invented arithmetic, letters, and numbers. Socrates also held the Egyptians in high regard and claimed that Solon traveled to Egypt in order to refine his own knowledge.

Egypt certainly had one of the oldest political systems in the world, and Aristotle claimed that Egypt was the original land of wisdom. During the Greco-Roman period, Egypt retained its reputation as a land of wisdom, and Alexandria became home to scholars from all over the world. These scholars worked at the Library of Alexandria and contributed to its contents. Unfortunately, the library was neglected during Roman rule and destroyed by a series of fires, which led to the loss of immense knowledge. While Alexandria remained an intellectual center, its influence declined as time passed.

Chapter 6: Medieval Egypt (650–1520 CE)

Ancient Egyptian history is filled with stories of mighty pharaohs who made their empire a glittering world power. Unfortunately, the pharaohs were unable to hold onto their power, which allowed Egypt to be ruled by several foreign dynasties. By the time Alexander the Great reached Egypt, the age of pyramids and powerful autonomous pharaohs was over. Over the next few centuries, Egypt would pass from the Greeks to the Romans before eventually becoming a part of the Byzantine Empire.

However, Egypt was soon lost to the Byzantine Empire when it was conquered by the Sasanid dynasty. In time, Egypt experienced another major upheaval when it was conquered by the Islamic Rashidun Caliphate. This period kickstarted the medieval era, which was marked by foreign Islamic kings who ruled over Egypt. The medieval era was a time of great change, advancement, and discovery for Egypt, but there were also periods of war and devastation.

Sasanian Egypt

For years, Egypt served as a province under the Byzantine Empire; however, the empire met troubled times when Maurice ascended to the throne around 582. Maurice had a difficult reign that was beset by war. At that time, Persia was ruled by the Sasanian dynasty; this empire is also referred to as the Neo-Persian Empire. Although Maurice was a successful military commander, he pushed his troops too far and was overthrown by Phocas and executed in 602. This event sparked massive unrest within the Byzantine Empire. The Persian shah at the time, Khosrow II, seized this opportunity and began conquering Byzantine lands, including northern Mesopotamia, Palestine, and Syria. In 618, Khosrow II invaded Egypt and conquered Alexandria.

After Alexandria fell, the rest of Egypt was conquered by the Persians, and by 621, Egypt had become a Persian province. The initial invasion of Egypt led to severe damage and losses, but once the Persians were in control, they began rebuilding parts of the country. While Egypt had become part of a different empire, the Sasanians used many of the same administrative policies as the Byzantine Empire. Some Iranian families even settled in the country, which means the two civilizations may have coexisted peacefully.

General Shahrbaraz governed Egypt on behalf of the Persian shah. A few years later, Heraclius, the Byzantine emperor, defeated the Persians, who left Egypt in 629. While the Byzantine Empire was able to regain Egypt, the empire had been weakened by the loss of its key territories and would struggle to hold onto many of its provinces.

The Muslim Conquest of Egypt

The Byzantine Empire managed to hold onto Egypt for another decade before Egypt was invaded again. In 639, the Rashidun Caliphate led a force over the Egyptian border. The army was made up of Roman and Persian soldiers who had converted to Islam. The

Rashidun army laid siege to Pelusium, which lasted for about two months. Meanwhile, the invading army had been joined by many Sinai Bedouins, which boosted its numbers. Many Egyptian cities were conquered or surrendered to the invading forces. The Byzantines and Muslims clashed at the Battle of Heliopolis, where the Byzantine army was soundly defeated. In 641, the Rashidun forces set out for Alexandria. The Byzantine forces managed to delay the Muslims' advance, but the invaders soon reached Alexandria.

The Byzantine Empire sent a massive army to defend the city, which led to the siege of Alexandria in 641. Alexandria wasn't an easy city to conquer, and the Byzantine army had installed catapults on the city's walls to protect it from invaders. It was a difficult siege, but the Muslims defeated the Byzantine army, and Alexandria surrendered. When the Muslims marched into Alexandria, they found a magnificent city that boasted palaces, places of entertainment, and massive amounts of wealth. Egypt was very rich, and its loss carried serious consequences for the Byzantine Empire. The Mediterranean had been known as the Roman Lake, but it was now being slowly divided between the Byzantine Empire and the Muslim caliphate. While the Muslims had conquered the Persian Empire, the Byzantines were able to resist invasion due to Constantinople's extensive fortifications.

The Rashidun Caliphate

Prophet Muhammad was the most influential Muslim leader who set the example for Islamic leadership and left behind a large number of Ansar. Their duties included ensuring that the caliphs paid close attention to the Quran and the Sunnah. The Rashidun were the first four leaders (caliphs) of the Muslim community. As caliphs, the Rashidun were responsible for leading prayers at the mosque, delivering sermons, and commanding the army. The Rashidun expanded the borders of the Islamic state to Iraq, Palestine, Iran, Armenia, Syria, and Egypt. They also instituted the

Islamic calendar and strengthened the Islamic community through religious studies. During the Rashidun Caliphate, the Islamic state conquered large portions of territory, which eventually became difficult to control. It was clear they would have to implement more practical administrative policies, as theocracy alone wasn't enough to rule the various regions.

Territories of the Rashidun Caliphate.
Mohammad adil at English Wikipedia, CC BY-SA 3.0
http://creativecommons.org/licenses/by-sa/3.0/, via Wikimedia Commons;
https://commons.wikimedia.org/wiki/File:Mohammad_adil_rais-rashidun_empire-at-its_peak.PNG

The first Rashidun caliph was Abu Bakr, who used the title of "Khalifat rasul Allah," which was eventually shortened to *khalifa* and became caliph. Abu Bakr was succeeded by Umar, who created a committee that would be in charge of choosing his successor in 644. The committee chose Uthman ibn Affan to be the next caliph, but his reign was marked by accusations of nepotism since his tribe, the Banu Umayyad, was allowed to gain significant influence. Uthman chose family members to rule conquered territories. Uthman was assassinated in 656 by Egyptian rebels, and the caliphate was offered to Ali ibn Abi Talib.

Ali was assassinated in 661, and his son, Hasan, was appointed as caliph but was challenged by Muawiya, who eventually became caliph instead of Hasan. The Rashidun Caliphate ended with Ali, and the Islamic territories came under the control of the Umayyad

Caliphate under Muawiya. Under the Umayyads, the role of caliph became the same as the role of a secular king.

Life in Early Islamic Egypt

When the Muslim forces invaded Egypt, they established a center near Babylon called Fustat, which became the seat of the governor and an administrative center. Soon after the invasion was complete, Egypt was divided into Upper and Lower Egypt again, as this made the territory easier to control. However, Caliph Uthman soon reunited Egypt under one governor who was to reside in Fustat. The governor would be responsible for taking care of Egypt, and he was allowed to appoint men to control Upper and Lower Egypt.

Artwork from Fustat.
https://commons.wikimedia.org/wiki/File:Seated_drinker,_from_a_bath_complex_in_Fustat.jpg

The Muslims had a strong military force that was mostly made up of Arab settlers and soldiers. An elite class made up of men quickly formed and enjoyed significant privileges. Many of the old systems of administration, including taxation, were kept in place, which would have helped the transition of power. Many Egyptians remained Christian and were allowed to practice their religion freely. As long as they provided tribute to the army, they were exempt from military service. At that time, conversions to Islam were still somewhat rare.

The Abbasid Caliphate

The Umayyad dynasty was overthrown by the Abbasid dynasty in 750. During the Umayyad dynasty, non-Arab Muslims, or mawali, were seen as lower class, which caused a lot of friction. When the Abbasids took power, they gave great favor to the mawali and accused the Umayyad caliphs of being immoral and unfit to rule. The Abbasids welcomed Persians to their court and moved their capital from Damascus to Baghdad, which won the approval of their mawali supporters. The Abbasids were descendants of Muhammad's uncle, Abbas ibn Abd al-Muttalib, who won the support of Shia Muslims. (Islam split into two factions, the Sunni and Shia, following the succession crisis after Muhammad's death.) Once the Abbasids began ruling, however, they switched allegiance back to the Sunni Muslims.

The Abbasid dynasty ruled for over three hundred years and accomplished impressive feats, such as strengthening Islamic rule, which then led to the Golden Age of Islam. This period is known as a time of great scientific, economic, and cultural advancements in Islamic culture. During the Abbasid dynasty, the office of vizier and elected local emirs (title of a high office within the Muslim community) gave certain men incredible influence. In time, caliphs became ceremonial positions while viziers exerted greater power. This led to the decline of the Abbasid Caliphate. During the 860s, Egypt founded the Tulunid Emirate, which was led by Ahmad ibn

Tulun. This emirate ruled separately from the caliphate. The Tulunids managed to control much of Egypt, Palestine, and the Hijaz (a region in western Saudi Arabia).

In 909, the Shia Ubayd Allah al-Mahdi Billah declared himself the caliph, which began a new caliphate in North Africa. This new caliphate was ruled by the Fatimid dynasty, who were the descendants of one of Muhammad's daughters.

The Fatimid Caliphate

The Fatimid dynasty rejected the Abbasid dynasty as usurpers since they were controlled by Sunni Muslims who wanted to take control of the entire Islamic caliphate. However, the Fatimids were only able to secure North Africa and parts of the Middle East. While other caliphs had been happy to recognize the Abbasids and only wanted to control specific regions, the Fatimids were determined to create an entirely new caliphate. The Fatimids set themselves up along the coast of Tunisia, where they tried to conquer Egypt. It took them several decades, but they finally achieved their goal in 969. The Fatimids managed to conquer the Nile valley. From there, they took Sinai, Palestine, and southern Syria. The Fatimids based their empire in Egypt and never wavered in their goal to become the only Islamic caliphate.

At its peak, the Fatimid dynasty controlled Sicily, North Africa, parts of the Red Sea coast, Palestine, Syria, Yemen, Mecca, and Medina. The control of the holy cities was extremely important since it added incredible religious prestige to a Muslim ruler's reign. During the Fatimid rule, the overthrow of the Abbasid Caliphate was perhaps the most important mission, and the Shia rulers sent missionaries and agents into Abbasid territories to gain support and converts. By 1057, the Fatimids had expanded into the east and nearly managed to take control of Baghdad. However, the Fatimids ultimately failed in their ultimate mission since the Sunni branch of Islam was reluctant to adopt Shia doctrines. By the 12th century, the

Crusades had begun, which forced the Sunni and Shia to fight the invading Christians.

Egypt during the Fatimid Caliphate

When the Fatimids conquered Egypt, they built the city of Cairo, which was supposed to be the royal residence of the Fatimid caliph. Fustat remained the administrative capital of Egypt until 1169. Egypt thrived under the Fatimid rule since the dynasty developed trade routes and boosted the economy. Soon, Egypt's trading routes ran along the Mediterranean Sea and the Indian Ocean and went as far as China. The Fatimids practiced religious tolerance, allowing Christians and Jews to live peacefully in Egypt. They also placed a high emphasis on ability over nepotism, which meant that anyone could rise quickly within the government if they had the skills.

The Fatimids kept a massive army of Mamluks (slaves), which allowed the Mamluks to become an elite class of knights and warriors. Some Mamluks became sultans and were allowed to hold positions of power. Besides the economy, the Fatimid caliphs also encouraged intellectual pursuits and built sophisticated libraries. They promoted freedom of thought, which allowed scholars to express their thoughts and views without fear of persecution. Once again, Egypt became a center of knowledge, philosophy, and literature. Scholars came from all over the world to benefit from this exchange of knowledge and praised Egypt's great libraries. The Fatimid caliphs were patrons of many scholars and appointed these scholars to prominent positions within their court. Unfortunately, the Fatimid dynasty declined during the 11th century, which allowed Saladin to invade Egypt in 1171.

Saladin was the founder of the Ayyubid dynasty, which led to the return of Fatimid lands to the Abbasid Caliphate.

The Black Death in Egypt

Before we dig into Saladin and the political situation in Egypt, let us take a look at an important event that occurred during the medieval age. The Black Death was a pandemic of bubonic plague that took place from 1346 to 1353 and caused up to seventy-five million to two hundred million deaths in Eurasia and North Africa. It's likely that the Black Death first started in Central Asia, but the first evidence of the pandemic was traced to Crimea in 1347. From there, the plague was carried by fleas that infested rats on trading vessels, which allowed the plague to be transported throughout the known world. It spread through the Mediterranean Basin to Africa, West Asia, and Europe. Once people caught the plague, it spread quickly, which caused the plague to spread to areas that could not be reached by trading vessels. Experts have theorized that the Black Death caused the world's population to go from around 475 million to around 350 to 375 million.

The pandemic caused the death of millions of people, which had a lasting effect on many civilizations. Since many areas experienced serious depopulation, the plague caused social, religious, and economic changes. The Black Death reached Alexandria around 1347 when an infected merchant ship carrying slaves arrived from Constantinople. By the next year, the plague had reached Cairo, which was the largest city in the Mediterranean Basin, as well as the cultural center of the Islamic community. According to some estimates, the plague decimated about 40 percent of Egypt's population. Before the plague, Cairo had about 600,000 inhabitants, and the Black Death killed about a third of the city's population. While the city had a functioning hospital, the severity of the plague and the sheer number of infected people overwhelmed the city's resources. The Nile was reportedly clogged with dead bodies because grave diggers and practitioners of funeral rites couldn't keep up with the demand.

The devastating effects of the Black Death differed according to geographical locations. Crowded urban centers were the most affected areas, but that doesn't mean rural towns were exempt from the tragedy.

The Mamluk Sultanate

Mamluks were slave soldiers who formed an elite fighting class in Egypt and later in the Ottoman Empire. They first served the Abbasid caliphs and were usually Turkic non-Muslims who had been captured in regions north of the Black Sea, now modern-day Russia. These soldiers converted to Islam and were tasked with protecting and serving caliphs, although they eventually became extremely powerful, especially in Egypt. Mamluks were trained as cavalry soldiers and had a code of conduct called the *furusiyya*, which encouraged values such as courage and generosity. Each Mamluk went through extensive training, which ensured that Mamluk forces were always ready to fight.

When Saladin conquered much of the Middle East, he founded the powerful Ayyubid dynasty. When he died, his heirs fought over control of his vast empire. Each of his heirs employed large retinues of Mamluk forces in the hopes of taking the empire for themselves. Saladin's brother, Al-Adil, finally managed to secure the whole empire after defeating his brothers and nephews and adding their Mamluk retinues to his own. The Ayyubids continued this practice until they were completely surrounded by the Mamluks, who eventually became an essential part of the Ayyubid court.

In 1250, Egyptian Sultan Turanshah died, causing his wife, Shajar al-Durr, to take power with Mamluk support. However, she needed a male counterpart, so she married a Mamluk commander named Aybak during the Seventh Crusade. Aybak was later assassinated, and a Mamluk named Qutuz took power and formed the Mamluk Sultanate, which would rule Egypt until around 1517 when it was defeated by the Ottoman Empire.

The Ottoman-Mamluk War

In 1453, Constantinople fell to the Ottoman Empire, which would bring the Ottomans into contact with the Mamluks. The two powers struggled for a monopoly on the highly lucrative spice trade.

The Ottomans conquered many regions in the Middle East, including the Islamic holy cities, and they had their eyes on Egypt.

The Mamluks responded by drafting people from rural areas to join their army, but this led to a shortage of food and necessary supplies since there weren't enough people to keep up the work on the farms. This shortage led to a famine that severely weakened Egypt. The Ottomans and Mamluks eventually went to war in 1516, and while both armies had around the same numbers, the Ottomans had a clear advantage. Only a small portion of the Mamluk army was trained soldiers, and they fought with outdated weapons such as bows and arrows. The Ottomans had a battle-hardened army equipped with modern weapons such as the arquebus. The Mamluks were incredibly proud and chose to rely on traditional methods, which led to their downfall. The Ottomans won the war in 1517 and took control of Egypt. Despite their defeat, the Mamluks were allowed to continue as a slave-soldier class but never regained the power and status they enjoyed during the Mamluk Sultanate.

The Ottomans placed a governor in Egypt, who was then protected by a highly trained force of Ottoman soldiers. Thanks to their victory in Egypt, the Ottomans were able to launch attacks on other African kingdoms, expanding their borders further. Thanks to their military victories, the Ottomans had control of the Islamic holy cities, which made the Ottoman rulers the caliphs over the entire Muslim world, including Egypt. They would hold onto that distinction until the 20th century.

Chapter 7: Early Modern Egypt (1520–1914 CE)

Egypt's medieval history was filled with wars, deadly plagues, and ever-shifting governments that had a powerful effect on the country and its people. During that time, the national religion changed several times, as the Egyptians went from a traditional pagan religion to Christianity and then to Islam. Besides affecting the Egyptian populace, these changing religions also had an effect on legal, economic, and administrative policies. The medieval period started with the Sasanid invasion and ended with the Ottoman invasion, which made Egypt a part of the Ottoman Empire. This change in government led to the beginning of Egypt's early modern period, which would last until the First World War.

While the early modern period was several centuries shorter than the medieval period, it was no less exciting. During the early modern period, Egypt had to adjust to life under the rule of the Ottomans, which contributed to the decline of Egypt's economy and culture. Egypt would also survive a terrible famine, weak and powerful rulers, a French invasion, the arrival of the British, and economic turmoil as foreign forces meddled in Egyptian affairs. All these events helped to shape Egyptian culture as the country left behind the medieval era and began its journey to modernity.

The Ottoman Empire

When the Ottomans took over Egypt, the country once again became a province. The Ottomans ruled from Constantinople and used Egypt as a granary and a source of income, which they obtained through taxation. Unfortunately, Egypt had begun to decline under the rule of the Mamluks, and the Ottoman invasion did little to help Egypt's economic position. As a result of the economic decline, Egypt's culture took a hit and began a steady decline. However, the Ottomans weren't solely responsible for these changes, as the Ottomans instituted several policies to ensure that they benefited from Egypt's prosperity. However, Egypt's elite class often didn't work with the government, which would have impacted the Ottomans' attempts to revive the economy.

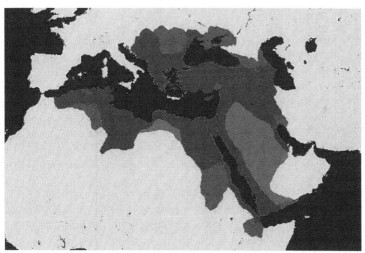

Map of the Ottoman Empire at its peak.
Dodobondo, CC BY-SA 4.0 https://creativecommons.org/licenses/by-sa/4.0 via Wikimedia Commons; https://commons.wikimedia.org/wiki/File:Ottoman-Empire-peak-1590-map.jpg

The Ottomans were quick to establish their authority in Egypt, and in 1525, Suleiman the Magnificent appointed a grand vizier, Ibrahim Pasha, who was responsible for ruling Egypt on behalf of his monarch. Ibrahim appointed a viceroy and a council of advisors who would be supported by a sizeable army. The Ottomans also separated Egypt into four manageable provinces, which would be assigned to inspectors who would oversee administration and taxation. The Egyptian government was controlled by officials from Constantinople, but in time, the Mamluks were able to obtain positions within the government.

Once the Ottomans established their authority in Egypt, they set their sights on expanding their borders farther south. Egypt was the perfect base for their new invasions, and soon, the Ottomans were able to control Nubia. They also fought the Portuguese for control of the Red Sea. They established a colony at Mitsiwa (modern-day Eritrea) and conquered Yemen and Aden. The Ottoman Empire was primarily Muslim, and they used their religion as the basis of many functions of government.

The Mamluk Elite

The Mamluks had long been an important class in Egypt. At first, they were simply a slave-warrior class, but in time, they developed into one of the most important classes in Egyptian society. While they lost much of their power after losing the Ottoman-Mamluk War, they were still allowed to exist in Egyptian society under the Ottoman Empire. In time, the Ottomans appointed Mamluks to act as inspectors or *kashifs* of specific Egyptian provinces. The Egyptian army also had a large number of Mamluks called the Circassian Mamluks. The Mamluks were able to work their way into higher offices within the government, and eventually, the Mamluks were part of the viceroy's advisory council.

Over time, the Mamluks were once again able to establish themselves as a powerful political and military power. The Mamluks retained many of their old practices to strengthen their ranks. The elite Mamluks would buy slaves and then train them according to the Mamluk traditions. Once the slave was trained, they were incorporated into the Mamluk household before being granted their freedom. By the 17th century, elite Mamluks served as beys. A bey was usually the governor of a province (or an equally important position). Beys were given salaries by the Ottoman Empire. While the Mamluks still paid tribute to the Ottomans and were overseen by the viceroy, they were essentially the most powerful class in Egypt. By the 18th century, the title of shaykh al-balad was created, which meant chief of the city. This title was given to the strongest bey. Eventually, two emirs, Ali Bey and Abu al-Dahab, were able to establish independent power. In 1786, the Ottomans tried to conquer the Mamluks but were forced to withdraw their army a year later. The Mamluks set up a coalition of two rulers (Murad Bey and Ibrahim Bey), which ruled Egypt until 1798.

Egyptian Culture during the Ottoman Empire

Egypt experienced a culture boom during the rule of the Mamluks and the Fatimid dynasty. Important individuals of those ruling powers made a habit of supporting scholars. This resulted in a surge of historians who documented events and left behind diligent records of the time periods in which they lived. However, during the Ottoman Empire, the Ottomans didn't place as much emphasis on education, knowledge, and culture. The Mamluk period, in particular, produced a high number of important historians, while only one significant Egyptian historian emerged during the reign of the Ottomans.

Egypt had been the home of international scholars and had been an intellectual center, but under the Ottoman Empire, the country lost that influence and prestige. The decline of Egyptian culture during this period is obvious in the lack of noteworthy public buildings that were constructed by the Ottomans. The Byzantine Basilica became a popular blueprint for mosques. And few advances were made in Egyptian architecture since architects were commissioned to recreate replicas or imitate building practices from Constantinople. During the Ottoman Empire, Egypt remained a primarily Muslim country, but Christians and Jews were permitted to practice their religion as long as they paid tribute to the Ottomans. However, this treatment varied throughout the empire's history.

The Famine of 1784

For most of its history, Egypt relied on the Nile for water and irrigation. The Nile was the source of life, and its regular flooding and water cycles fertilized the soil and allowed farmers to harvest a massive amount of food. Unfortunately, this dependence also meant that if the Nile didn't flood or if it was affected by a drought, the entire country suffered. In 1783, the Nile didn't rise like it was supposed to, which meant that many farms didn't have enough water for their fields and crops. There was also a lack of seeds, which meant that farmers fell behind with their work. The same conditions persisted the next year, which plunged Egypt into a severe famine. Experts estimate that the famine caused the population of Egypt to drop by one-sixth. It was the worst disaster to affect Egypt since the Black Death a few centuries earlier.

Since the famine occurred while the Ottoman Empire was ruling Egypt, it is seen as one of the ways the Ottomans failed Egypt since so many Egyptians died. A study conducted in recent years by Rutgers and funded by the National Science Foundation and the National Aeronautics and Space Administration (NASA) showed that an eruption of an Icelandic volcano may have been responsible for the Nile's low flow during 1783. Since the Egyptian economy relied heavily on the Nile, the change in the Nile's flow had disastrous consequences for the economy.

The French Invasion

In the 17th and 18th centuries, France periodically investigated the possibility of occupying Egypt. However, when Napoleon Bonaparte sailed for Egypt in 1798, he was thinking specifically of using Egypt to strike a blow against Britain. If he managed to accomplish his goal, he would be able to curb Britain's trade routes and be in a better position to negotiate a peace treaty with the British. The French were also looking into the possibility of helping Egypt return to its ancient glory, which would have positive consequences for France since they would benefit greatly from Egypt's potential wealth. When Napoleon's forces set off for Egypt, they were joined by scientists who were tasked with creating a report on Egypt's condition and resources.

The first challenge the fleet faced was the British Mediterranean fleet, which was commanded by Horatio Nelson. Since France and Britain were at war, if the French fleet was caught, it would have to survive a naval battle, which would weaken its chances of occupying Egypt. Napoleon was able to navigate his fleet to Egyptian shores without attracting the attention of the British navy and landed at Aboukir Bay on July 1st. The next day, the French took Alexandria. Napoleon issued a proclamation in Arabic, assuring the Egyptians that he planned to overthrow the Mamluks. He also promised that he had no problems with Islam or the Ottomans. When Napoleon addressed his men, he promised to give them land in Egypt but warned them not to disrespect the Muslims since they would be living among them. The Egyptians were skeptical of Napoleon's promises, and the French invasion would soon meet serious challenges.

Napoleon in Egypt

As soon as Napoleon conquered Alexandria, he mobilized his army and marched toward Cairo. However, the Mamluks weren't about to give up that easily, and Murad Bey led an army against Napoleon at Shubra Khit on July 13th. Napoleon won the battle, and the armies met again at the Battle of the Pyramids on July 21st. The French were attacked by the Mamluks, who controlled an army of about six thousand men. Napoleon defeated the Mamluks and took Cairo on July 25th. Murad Bey was forced to flee to Upper Egypt while Ibrahim Bey retreated to Syria.

Napoleon in Egypt.
https://commons.wikimedia.org/wiki/File:Napoleon_in_Egypt_by_Jean-Leon_Gerome,_French,_1867-1868,_oil_on_wood_panel_-_Princeton_University_Art_Museum_-_DSC07051.jpg

While Napoleon experienced great victories on land, the British navy was close to Egypt and would arrive at the end of the month. Napoleon didn't waste any time in Cairo and appointed a series of councils to advise him as he took control of the Egyptian government. For the first time in centuries, Egypt was once again introduced to the West; it had been sheltered by the Mamluks and Ottomans, who mostly focused on the East. The French succeeded in opening Egypt up to Europe. They also managed to weaken the Mamluk ruling force, which would never return to its former glory.

During the occupation, French scholars uncovered the Rosetta Stone, which bore trilingual carvings and helped scholars decipher hieroglyphs. It was an astounding discovery that would form the basis of Egyptology and expose Egypt's ancient culture to the modern world.

The early part of Napoleon's Egyptian campaign was successful, which may have bolstered French morale. However, the French and British would soon meet in a climactic naval battle that would turn the tide against Napoleon and cause him to return to France the next year.

The Battle of the Nile

When the British discovered that Napoleon planned to occupy Egypt, they sent Horatio Nelson to scout Napoleon's operations at Toulon. However, when Nelson arrived, he found the port was empty and that Napoleon had already left. Nelson correctly guessed what Napoleon wanted to do and headed to Alexandria, which was also empty. The British navy had arrived too early. Nelson sailed for Sicily. When he returned to Egypt in August, he found the French fleet at Aboukir Bay. The French fleet was commanded by Admiral François-Paul Brueys d'Aigailliers.

Battle of the Nile
https://commons.wikimedia.org/wiki/File:Loutherbourg_-_battle_of_the_nile.jpg

Nelson seized his opportunity and commanded the British forces to attack the French fleet at once. During the night, Napoleon suffered a head wound, and the French flagship, *L'Orient*, was destroyed by the British. Brueys was onboard at the time and died along with most of the sailors aboard. The French fleet was almost completely destroyed; only a handful of ships were able to escape. It was a devastating blow to Napoleon's army, and it was the beginning of the end of the French occupation.

It soon became apparent that the Egyptians were dissatisfied with French rule, as Napoleon had to deal with an uprising in Cairo in October 1798. The Ottoman sultan, Selim III, declared war on France in September. In August 1799, Napoleon left Egypt and returned to France, leaving Jean-Baptiste Kléber in charge. The French would be forced to surrender in 1801 when British forces landed at Aboukir. On top of this, the Ottomans advanced into Egypt from Syria, and the British-Indian army landed on the Red Sea coast.

Muhammad Ali of Egypt

Once the French left Egypt, the Ottomans were determined to recover Egypt. The British forces left Egypt in 1803, but the Ottomans still had to fight the remaining Mamluk factions that wanted to reassert their power. As a result, the Ottomans relied on an Albanian fighting force, which helped the Ottomans take back Egypt and appoint a viceroy who would protect Ottoman interests. However, the Albanians had their own plans and rebelled against the Ottomans. Their leader became the new viceroy, but he was quickly assassinated, which led to the appointment of his successor, Muhammad Ali, who overthrew the Mamluks and Ottomans.

Muhammad Ali was appointed as viceroy by the Ottoman sultan in an effort to end revolts that erupted in Cairo in 1805. The new viceroy proved to be a competent military leader who won several important battles. In 1807, the British tried to occupy Egypt in an effort to gain a strategic position over Napoleon's army. However,

Muhammad Ali defeated their expedition, and the British were forced to retreat. Since the Ottoman Empire was facing serious difficulties, he was allowed to separate himself from the empire, declare himself Egypt's leader, and conquer vast amounts of lands that had previously been controlled by the Ottomans. Afterward, he expanded Egypt's territories to central Arabia and northern Sudan, which allowed him to take advantage of a lucrative slave trade route. Unfortunately, Muhammad Ali's Arabian Empire fell apart during his lifetime, but he continued ruling over Egypt.

As Egypt's leader, he modernized the Egyptian Army, boosted the economy, encouraged education, and founded several educational institutions. He sent several Egyptians to French universities, which separated Egypt from the Ottoman culture. Muhammad Ali also introduced vaccinations for children, forced labor, and military conscriptions. He turned Egypt into a coercive state. The Egyptians weren't happy under Muhammad Ali's rule, and there were several peasant revolts, all of which were quickly subdued. In 1848, Muhammad Ali had become senile, and his son, Ibrahim, took control of Egypt. Ibrahim ruled for a few months before his death and was succeeded by his son, Abbās I. Muhammad Ali died in 1849.

Muhammad Ali

https://commons.wikimedia.org/wiki/File:ModernEgypt,_Muhammad_Ali_by_Auguste_C ouder,_BAP_17996.jpg

The Khedivate of Egypt

When the French were expelled from Egypt and Muhammad Ali founded his dynasty, Egypt became the Khedivate of Egypt. It was an autonomous state that was allowed to act independently but had to pay tribute to the Ottoman Empire. While Muhammad Ali managed to rule Egypt effectively for several decades, his successors struggled to do the same. In 1863, Ismail took the throne, and he was determined to modernize Egypt. Unfortunately, his lofty goals and extravagance led to bankruptcy, which resulted in European interference in Egypt's economy and development. Ismail managed to receive the title of khedive, which essentially made him an independent sovereign from the Ottoman Empire, but this privilege meant he had to pay more tribute to the Ottomans.

Ismail was brought increasingly under European control, and for some years, Egypt was ruled jointly by the French and British. In 1879, Ismail was forced out of office, and his son, Tewfik, was proclaimed khedive. However, a few years later, an officer named Ahmed 'Urabi caught wind of discontent among the army and lower classes. He quickly created a revolt against the Europeans and Turks. The government was unable to stop 'Urabi, and he quickly rose within the government and became a cabinet member. This wasn't enough for him, and soon, widespread revolts broke out.

In 1882, the British and French took their fleets to Alexandria to suppress the serious rebellion and protect European interests, but the French retreated. The British stayed, suppressing the revolt and installing their troops in Egypt. It was meant to be a temporary measure, but the British would remain in Egypt until 1956. 'Urabi was defeated and forced into exile, and the khedive was allowed to rule again. At first, the British government didn't establish formal political control in Egypt since they knew it would cause trouble with the Ottomans and other European nations. However, the British claimed to be protecting their interests in Egypt, which required their military presence in the country.

While the British never established their formal political presence in Egypt, they still had significant power in Egypt. For example, when Tewfik and his government placed 'Urabi and his conspirators on trial, the rebels were originally sentenced to death. However, the British interfered and commuted the rebels' sentences to exile. Tewfik formed his own cabinet, with Riaz Pasha acting as a leading member. However, after the British interference, Riaz quit, and the khedive worked with the British ambassador in Istanbul to reorganize the Egyptian government. During his time as khedive, Tewfik posed little resistance to British interference. However, when he died, he was succeeded by his son, Abbās II, in 1892. He wasn't as complacent as his father and would pose serious problems for the British.

Chapter 8: Late Modern Egypt (1890–2013 CE)

Once the British occupied Egypt, they began interfering with Egyptian politics, as they had invested heavily into the Egyptian economy and wanted to ensure that their investment was being protected. Unfortunately, their interference often didn't line up with Egypt's best interests, which led to conflict and enmity. While many of Muhammad Ali's successors worked with the British, that cooperation ended under the rule of Abbās II. Almost as soon as the British were finished dealing with Abbās II, another threat loomed on the horizon. When Britain declared war on the Ottoman Empire during World War I, Egypt became a base of operations, and it would suffer greatly during the war years.

Soon after the First World War, Egypt emerged as an independent kingdom before transforming into a republic. Finally free from foreign leadership, Egypt's government went through several transformations as new political groups sprang up and vied for dominance. Among these were the Wafd and the Muslim Brotherhood, which would both have a serious impact on modern Egyptian politics. In recent years, Egypt has also endured tumultuous events that shaped its government, people, and culture.

This new period in Egyptian history may not have the prestige of ancient Egypt, but it is still fascinating.

Abbās II

When Abbās II inherited the office of khedive from his father in 1892, there was growing resentment about British influence in Egypt. Unlike his father, Abbās wasn't willing to submit to British rule and almost immediately showed that he didn't appreciate British interference in his government. This won him the support of Egyptian nationalists, and Abbās appointed a prime minister who shared his views. Abbās also provided support for the *Al-Mu'ayyad*, which was an anti-British newspaper. After his loud criticism of the British, Lord Cromer, the British consul general in Egypt, decided that the khedive's influence was growing too strong.

However, in 1906, Egyptian nationalists declared they wanted a constitutional government, but Abbās denied their petition. The next year, the National Party was established, led by Mustafā Kāmil. By that time, Lord Cromer had been replaced by Lord Kitchener as consul general, and he took more serious steps to curb Abbās's independence. He also struck a blow to the National Party by exiling or imprisoning all its leaders.

Court of Shah Abbās II.
Credit: Sorosh Tavakoli from Stockholm, Sverige, CC BY 2.0
https://creativecommons.org/licenses/by/2.0 via Wikimedia Commons;
https://commons.wikimedia.org/wiki/File:Shah_Abbas_II.jpg

Abbās wasn't about to give up. He bided his time. His chance presented itself when World War I broke out, as the British were preparing to enter the fray. Abbās urged his supporters, the Egyptians and the Sudanese, to fight against the British occupation. Abbās's plan was to join the Central Powers (the coalition of the German Empire, the Ottoman Empire, and Austria-Hungary, which was at war with France, Britain, and Russia). However, Abbās's appeal failed, and he was deposed in 1914. He was replaced by his uncle, Husayn Kāmil, who became the first sultan of the British protectorate. Abbās II spent the rest of his life in exile.

World War I

In November 1914, Britain declared war on the Ottoman Empire. Since the khedive of Egypt was allied with the Ottomans, he was deposed, and a British protectorate was formed. While Egypt had no formal part in the war, it became a British base camp, and over a million Egyptians were drafted. According to sources from the time, the Egyptians suffered greatly in the war because they weren't given appropriate supplies, such as tents, food, and medical resources. Worse still, the forced conscription led to serious economic consequences that caused a recession and poverty in Egypt. During the war, the soldiers were treated worse than animals, and many of them died from foreign diseases and wounds.

The Egyptians were unaccustomed to conditions in France and died from cholera or the cold. When the soldiers returned, they were rewarded with little compensation, and disabled Egyptians weren't supported. They also brought foreign diseases, such as cholera, with them. The Egyptian medical system wasn't equipped for the onslaught of victims.

Due to its strategic position, Britain stationed troops in Egypt and made several fortifications in Egyptian cities, such as a giant cannon in Alexandria. Residents were forced to stay at home during certain hours due to raids. Public buildings were turned into hospitals, while British, Indian, and Australian troops were sent to

Egypt during their breaks. In order to support the war efforts, the Egyptians were forced to pay tribute to the British, which added to Egypt's financial strain. If the Egyptians failed to pay the levies, they would be placed under martial law. The British also ended Ottoman rule in Egypt, and when the Ottoman Empire fell, its lands were divided between Britain and France.

While the whole world was impacted by World War I, Britain took advantage of Egypt by forcing its citizens into the army and using its resources for its own gain. All of this led to widespread revolution in Egypt in 1919 and Egypt's eventual independence.

The Wafd

As World War I raged on, Egyptians became increasingly unhappy with British rule. As soon as the war ended, Egypt tried to claim complete independence from Britain. During this time, a delegation of notable Egyptians created the Wafd Party, which was a nationalist liberal political party. The Wafd Party was led by Saad Zaghloul, who was an immensely popular and charismatic leader. For the next few years, the Wafd would be intimately involved in Egyptian politics, but it was only allowed to become a formal party in 1924.

Picture of the Wafd Party
https://commons.wikimedia.org/wiki/File:Blue_Shirts_(Wafd_party).jpg

The party was strictly organized according to a hierarchy, with the executive council at the top. They also had organizers who worked in cities and villages to create support for their cause. The Wafd was mostly made up of urban Egyptians who belonged to the upper and middle classes, but they quickly endeared themselves to most Egyptians who longed for freedom from the British. While Saad Zaghloul served as the party's president, there were also a number of prominent women among their ranks. Zaghloul's wife, Safiya, became an important voice in the struggle for women's rights, along with Huda Sha'arawi. Unfortunately, the Wafd faced serious challenges from the British and the Egyptian monarchy, which both sought to undercut the Wafd's influence.

Saad Zaghloul

Saad Zaghloul was born to a peasant family in the Nile River delta. His family made enough money to send him to the Al-Azhar University in Cairo, and he later attended the Egyptian School of Law. In and later married Safiya, the daughter of the Egyptian prime minister, Mustafa Pasha Fahmi. Safiya, like her husband, was active in politics and became an influential revolutionary and feminist. In 1906, Zaghloul became the head of the Ministry of Education. Around this time, Egyptian nationalism was on the rise, and Zaghloul helped create Hizb al-Umma, the People's Party.

Saad Zaghloul
https://commons.wikimedia.org/wiki/File:ModernEgypt,_Saad_Zaghloul,_BAP_14781.jpg

During Zaghloul's time in the government, he worked with British occupiers, which didn't win him any favors with the nationalists. However, by 1913, he had been elected to the Legislative Assembly and began criticizing the government and British involvement. When Egypt became a British protectorate, Egyptians suffered due to conscription, martial law, and inflation. It was becoming clear that the British were planning to turn Egypt into a colony, and the Egyptians were livid. During World War One, Zaghloul was busy forming various activist groups throughout the country.

On November 13th, 1918, Zaghloul led the Wafd to call upon the British high commissioner (the British representative in Egypt), Sir Reginald Wingate. They declared their intention to lead the Egyptians and demanded that the protectorate be replaced with a treaty of alliance. The Wafd wanted to negotiate this treaty directly with the British government, but their requests were denied. This led to widespread revolts in Egypt, known as the 1919 Revolution. In 1919, the leaders of the Wafd were arrested and exiled, which only infuriated the Egyptian populace further.

Wingate was immediately replaced with General Edmund Allenby, who released the Wafd leaders. Zaghloul then represented Egypt at the Peace Conference in Paris, and while his attempts were unsuccessful, he became a national hero. During the next few years, Zaghloul became increasingly popular. The British allowed a new constitution in 1923 (Egypt was allowed to become a constitutional monarchy), and in 1924, the Wafd won the general elections, making Zaghloul the new prime minister of Egypt. Zaghloul was immensely popular, but this popularity was only partly due to his charisma. His humble background endeared him to the Egyptian populace, and he became the catalyst of a movement that would outlive him.

The Egyptian Kingdom

After the 1919 Revolution, Britain realized its protectorate was failing and that new measures were needed. In 1922, the Unilateral Declaration of Egyptian Independence was negotiated, and the Kingdom of Egypt was established. However, this independence was only nominal, as the British were allowed to have some involvement in Egyptian politics, and British troops remained in Egypt. The kingdom was led by King Fuad I and later by his son, Farouk I.

During Zaghloul's later years, he agreed to form a coalition government with Lord Lloyd, the British high commissioner. When Zaghloul died in 1927, Mustafā al-Nahhās became the president of the Wafd. In 1936, he signed the Anglo-Egyptian Treaty, which allowed the British to keep their troops along the Suez Canal. The treaty also allowed the British to keep control of Sudan. Since radical fascism was on the rise in the 1930s, the Wafd created the Blue Shirts, a militant youth group.

The Effects of World War II

Egypt was forced to support Britain during World War II, but few Egyptians expected Britain to win. During the war, Italy aligned itself with Nazi Germany and declared war on Britain and France in June 1940. Egypt remained neutral, but due to the Anglo-Egyptian Treaty of 1936, the British were allowed to occupy the Suez Canal if it was threatened. It wasn't long before Italy began launching raids on Egypt from the Italian colony of Libya. The Italians tried to reach the Suez Canal but were stopped by the British before they could attain their objective.

In 1942, Germany nearly invaded Egypt, which caused Britain to interfere in the Egyptian government. In the 4 February Incident, King Farouk was forced to make al-Nahhās his prime minister. While this may have seemed like a victory for the Wafd, as they had succeeded in winning the elections in March 1942, it became clear that the Wafd weren't the champions of Egyptian nationalism anymore since Nahhās cooperated with the British.

World War II completely destabilized Egypt. As the Wafd declined, other political parties fought for dominance and called for a revision of the 1936 treaty. Egyptians wanted the British to withdraw their troops from the Suez Canal and end British control of Sudan. Extremists gained popularity, and groups like the Muslim Brotherhood committed violent activities and supported unrest. All of this led to a revolution that began in 1952. The revolution, which was led by Gamal Abdel Nasser, included a military coup that brought a sudden end to Egypt's constitutional monarchy. The revolution led to a time of profound political and social changes in Egypt. On June 18th, 1953, Egypt became a republic, with Mohamed Naguib as its first president.

The Muslim Brotherhood

The Muslim Brotherhood is Egypt's oldest political Islamic group, and it isn't allowed to operate as a political party in some countries. The group was founded in 1928 in Egypt by Hassan al-

Banna. The group was created because its founder dreamed of forming a system of Islamic rule that would be founded firmly on Islamic laws and principles. Hassan al-Banna thought he could achieve this dream by offering various social services to the people. Eventually, the Muslim Brotherhood set its sights on reforming all existing governments in the Arab world.

During its history, the Muslim Brotherhood has been accused of committing acts of violence and terrorism. At first, the Muslim Brotherhood focused on preaching Islam, setting up hospitals, boosting the economy, and teaching the illiterate. Since it was founded during a time when there was widespread unrest due to British occupation, it was only a matter of time before the Muslim Brotherhood entered the political arena.

The Muslim Brotherhood cooperated with the Free Officers (which was a group of revolutionary nationalist officers in the Egyptian Armed Forces) at first, but when there were differences of opinions between the groups, they stopped working together. In the 1950s, there was an assassination attempt on Gamal Abdel Nasser. This led to the imprisonment of Sayyid Qutb, who was a leading member of the Muslim Brotherhood. While in prison, he advocated the benefits of an armed struggle against the Egyptian regime. Eventually, he was executed, but his writings were still used by Islamist groups to advocate armed struggles. The Muslim Brotherhood agreed to abandon violence in the 1970s, and in 1995, they adopted democracy. Over time, the Muslim Brotherhood spread to other Arab countries and influenced various Islamic groups.

The Nasser Regime

Gamal Abdel Nasser was born in 1918 and participated in anti-British protests during his youth. After studying law for a few months, he entered the Royal Military Academy and graduated in 1938 as a second lieutenant. During World War II, he helped form a secret organization called the Free Officers. In 1952, the Free

Officers, led by Nasser, formed a coup that deposed King Farouk. Mohamed Naguib became the Egyptian prime minister in 1953, but Nasser removed Naguib from power in 1954 and became the new prime minister instead.

Nasser proved to be a popular and effective leader. In 1956, his new constitution and presidency were confirmed by the Egyptian voters. Nasser then made an arms agreement with the USSR, which caused the British to refuse to pay for Nasser's High Dam project that would be built across the Nile in Aswan, Egypt.

In response, Nasser nationalized the Suez Canal, which was technically owned by France and England. In October 1956, Israel, France, and Britain attacked Egypt. The foreign forces were able to occupy the Suez Canal but were pressured to retreat by the United Nations and Soviets. In 1957, the Suez Canal was completely under Egyptian control. In 1970, the Aswan High Dam was completed, which provided a massive boost to the Egyptian economy. Nasser was highly respected throughout the world, and his independent policies made him a beloved leader among the Egyptians. Two months after the completion of the Aswan High Dam, Nasser died of a heart attack and was succeeded by Anwar el-Sadat. Nasser's regime ended 2,300 years of foreign rule and introduced a new era in Egyptian history.

Anwar Sadat

Anwar el-Sadat was born in 1918 and graduated from the Cairo Military Academy in 1938. During World War II, he was arrested by the British for plotting to overthrow them. He managed to escape in 1950 and joined the Free Officers, helping Nasser to overthrow the monarchy. During Nasser's regime, Sadat held several positions in the government until he eventually became Nasser's vice president. When Nasser died, he became the president of Egypt in September 1970.

Anwar Sadat
Aboadel2020, CC BY-SA 4.0 https://creativecommons.org/licenses/by-sa/4.0 via Wikimedia Commons; https://commons.wikimedia.org/wiki/File:Anwar_Sadat.jpg

While Sadat upheld some of Nasser's policies at first, he quickly began setting himself apart from Nasser's legacy. He instituted a program of economic reforms that involved attracting foreign investment. His efforts weren't very successful; they led to inflation, the unequal distribution of wealth, and food riots in 1977. He famously ended Egypt's partnership with the Soviets. In 1973, he entered the Arab-Israeli War and retook some territories in Israel. However, Sadat soon began working toward peace in the Middle East and made a historic visit to Israel. Sadat also began negotiating for peace with Israel's prime minister, Menachem Begin, which resulted in the Camp David Accords, a preliminary peace treaty between the two countries. This action also earned Sadat and Begin a Nobel Peace Prize in 1978. In 1979, Sadat succeeded in obtaining a treaty of peace between Israel and Egypt.

Unfortunately, not everyone supported the peace treaty, which led to opposition within Sadat's government. The economy was also worsening, which caused public unrest. In September 1981, Sadat fought back by imprisoning 1,500 of his opponents from every walk of life. The next month, he was assassinated by the Egyptian Islamic Jihad, a militant Islamist group. Sadat was succeeded by Hosni Mubarak in 1981, who would serve as president for three decades.

The Egyptian Crisis

On January 25th, 2011, Egyptian youths felt compelled to protest against Hosni Mubarak's regime in Cairo. Crowds gathered in Tahrir Square to protest rising poverty and unemployment. The protests lasted for eighteen days and quickly became a revolution. Egypt descended into violence, repression, and a political deficit. The aim of the protests was to overthrow Hosni Mubarak. While Mubarak was removed from office during the revolution, things quickly got worse when political parties fought against the Muslim Brotherhood for dominance. Hundreds of protestors were killed during the revolution, which only added to the frustration and unrest.

In June 2012, Mohamed Morsi won Egypt's democratic elections and became prime minister. However, the unrest in Egypt was far from over. Morsi's presidency was marked by diplomatic, economic, and security challenges, as well as energy shortages. In 2013, Abdel Fattah al-Sisi led a coup that overthrew Morsi, allowing him to become the president of Egypt.

PART THREE: Egyptian Society Through the Ages

Chapter 9: Society and Its Structure

Egypt underwent many changes during its long history. The region developed from separate scattered tribes into a highly organized empire with an intricate religious system. During ancient Egypt, society had a pyramid-like structure, with the pharaoh and gods at the top and slaves forming the wide base of Egyptian society. When the Egyptians came under foreign rule, they were subjected to the traditions, cultures, and social structures of various other countries. As the spread of Christianity became prevalent, Egyptian society underwent more changes, as the pagan priestly classes were replaced by monks.

While Coptic Orthodox Christians remained in Egypt, the vast majority of people eventually adopted Islam, which once again changed the traditional social structure. Over the years, Egyptian society adapted and formed its own unique identity that stood apart from other Islamic kingdoms, especially when the Mamluks took over. These changes affected everything from laws to clothing.

Ancient Egyptian Society

The most important value of ancient Egyptian society was ma'at, which signified harmony and balance. If ma'at wasn't preserved, it was believed that society would collapse into chaos. One way to preserve ma'at was by maintaining the social balance, which is why the intermediate periods were seen as periods of lawlessness and chaos. The social order broke down during Egypt's various intermediate periods, which caused scholars and historians to describe these ages as dark times. The ancient Egyptian social hierarchy was shaped like a pyramid with the king at the top. After the king came his vizier and courtiers, followed by the scribes and priests. Next came the nomarchs (or regional governors). After the nomarchs came the generals, then artists and supervisors of worksites. At the bottom were the peasants and slaves.

Pyramid of Egyptian society.

In ancient Egypt, the gods reigned supreme, and the people believed that the gods had created them and placed them in a perfect home. They believed that the gods appointed a ruler whose primary responsibility was representing the gods' will to the people and preserving the all-important ma'at. If the pharaoh was able to fulfill their duties, then everything would work as it should. Since the social order was so intricately tied to religion, social mobility wasn't an option. People couldn't easily climb ranks or switch to a different class since this would upset the natural order of things.

Since the pharaoh had so many duties, the position of vizier was created to help them. The vizier took care of many of the practical duties of administration, such as delegating duties, overseeing the governors and military, tax collection, and checking on the ruler's building projects. The peasant farmers made up the vast majority of the population, although the slave class was an integral part of Egyptian society. Slaves were usually criminals, people who couldn't pay their debts, or prisoners of war.

Ancient Egyptian Law

Tradition was extremely important in Egyptian culture, and the ancient Egyptians promoted strict obedience to the natural order of things, including the legal system. The Egyptians had developed their own legal system as early as the Predynastic period, which stretched from around 6000 to 3150 BCE. As Egypt developed, so did its laws. Once again, ma'at came heavily into play, as most of the Egyptian legal system revolved around preserving ma'at. The Egyptians believed that people needed help to stay on the path set out by the gods. If someone disobeyed those laws, they were punished severely, as everyone understood that keeping to the laws was within everyone's best interests. Unfortunately, this meant that the Egyptians often believed that people were guilty unless it could be proven otherwise. If a person was accused of committing a crime, they would likely be punished, although there were isolated cases of leniency.

Although no official law codes have been found in Egypt, it's clear that the Egyptians followed a legal system because legal precedents already existed by the time of the Early Dynastic period (3150-2613 BCE). It seems that laws were enforced by police officers who were tasked with keeping the peace. If a criminal was caught, they would face the judicial system. The ancient Egyptians believed that their laws were handed down from the gods at the moment of creation, which made the king the head of the judicial system. The vizier usually had a say in judicial matters but could be overruled by the king. Viziers typically appointed magistrates and could be prevailed upon to get involved in local courts, but these instances were rare. Nomarchs would also be responsible for ensuring that justice was dispensed within their districts. There is some evidence that priests acted as judges in certain cases, as the people believed they could consult with the gods to receive an accurate judgment.

Adultery was a serious offense, and both husbands and wives were allowed to take their spouses to court if their infidelities were exposed. Families were extremely important to maintain ma'at and social balance. A woman guilty of infidelity could be divorced, have her nose amputated, or be burned to death. While a man could receive up to one thousand blows, he wouldn't face the death penalty. The judicial system relied heavily on the testimonies of witnesses, which meant that false witnesses were given incredibly harsh sentences. However, in most cases, public disgrace was a terrible enough prospect that most people tended to obey the laws. Ancient Egyptians relied heavily on their communities, so public humiliation or ostracization would have been a terrible fate for any family.

Daily Life in Ancient Egypt

Everyone had their designated place in ancient Egypt, and people were generally proud of their work. They believed they were fulfilling their roles within the natural order and were contributing to keeping the balance of things intact. It is believed that ancient artisans and workmen volunteered their time and skills to a king's building project. For years, it was believed that the pyramids were completed with slave labor, and while slaves certainly helped build the monuments, the king's public projects were a source of national pride, which drew free men to offer their services too.

Family formed the basis of Egyptian society, and tomb offerings were made to the deceased. If a family didn't have time to present the offerings themselves, they could hire priests to make offerings on their behalf.

The ancient Egyptians were extremely clean and took time to groom themselves. Farmers wove flax into fine linen. Peasants and working men wore long garments tied with a sash at the waist, as well as short kilts. Rich men wore knee-length shirts and kilts with jewelry and makeup. Many Egyptians went barefoot, but many also wore papyrus sandals. Working-class women wore long wrap-around dresses, while wealthy women were able to wear elaborate adornments with their dresses. Jewelry usually consisted of beads, armlets, bracelets, necklaces, and earrings.

Daily Life in Ptolemaic Egypt

By the time the Ptolemies ruled Egypt, the country had already been influenced by the Hellenistic culture and religion. The pyramid-like structure of society had broken down, with most of the important positions in the government being given to Greeks or Greek descendants. The Ptolemies kept the Egyptian religion, but the country was becoming increasingly diverse. The Egyptians were allowed to follow their own traditions and laws, but the Greeks were governed according to Greek laws, which meant that life in Egypt differed according to a person's lineage.

When Alexander the Great conquered Egypt, he made it a part of his ethnically diverse empire. This meant that Egypt was opened up to different cultures, with many people moving into Egypt and bringing their cultures with them. Cities like Alexandria became cosmopolitan melting pots of cultures, religions, and intellectual theories. While the Egyptian religion was allowed to continue, the Greeks brought new practices of worship and soon blended the Egyptian and Greek religions together.

The Ptolemies owned most of the land in Egypt, and farmers were subjected to government control, which allowed the Ptolemies to grow richer. Although taxes rose and oversight increased, the government sponsored irrigation projects that helped to boost the economy. Egypt participated in trade with many foreign countries, and port cities were given access to exotic luxury goods. Since the Greeks prized education, wealthy women were educated and allowed to participate in certain religious rites. Unfortunately, Egypt's fertility and grain production made it an irresistible prize to the Roman Empire, and soon, Egyptian society changed again.

Roman Influences on Egyptian Society

While the Ptolemies kept themselves apart from the Egyptians, they still remained in Egypt during their rule. However, when Egypt became a Roman state, the Roman emperor allied himself with the pharaohs but ruled from Rome. The first Roman emperor, Augustus, appointed a governor who controlled the region and reported back to the emperor. Egypt became the home to Roman legions until Augustus was sure the Egyptians wouldn't rebel. The Romans changed the laws in Egypt so that they conformed to Roman laws, and business was conducted according to Roman procedures. The local administration also changed to the Roman system and dictated that landowners were responsible for carrying out public services and had to take care of their lands.

Once again, special privileges were reserved for Greek and Roman citizens. As Rome's breadbasket, Egypt had to supply Rome with grain, and its natural resources were used for the good of the Roman Empire. However, it would seem that the Egyptians also had an impact on the Romans, as Roman architecture bore resemblances of Egyptian styles. The Egyptians were also exposed to new ideas, as Alexandria attracted many notable scholars. Meanwhile, daily life in rural areas stayed mostly the same, although the wealthy were expected to contribute to society, and everyone was governed according to Roman laws.

Byzantine Social Structure

When the Roman Empire was split into two distinct sections, Egypt fell under the Byzantine Empire, which soon developed its own identity that distinguished it from the Western Roman Empire. Byzantine society was controlled by the royal family and the wealthy elite. However, unlike in ancient Egypt, social mobility was much more frequent, as people could advance due to wars, imperial favor, land ownership, or intermarriage. Ordinary people likely adopted their parents' profession, but ambitious individuals could realistically hope to advance their social standing.

The Byzantine Empire was also astonishingly diverse, and its cities became incredibly cosmopolitan. Alexandria was allowed to gain influence again and was the gateway for merchants, refugees, mercenaries, pilgrims, and travelers. Byzantine society was still somewhat stratified and consisted of two main classes: the privileged (*honestiores*) and the humble (*humiliores*), which basically meant the rich and everyone else. Slaves had their own social class, but this class was lower than all the others. This social divide meant there was a definite difference in standards of living. The rich had more than enough to survive and still live lavishly, while the poor struggled to make a living. However, the wealthy class didn't depend on blood or descendancy anymore since dynasties changed quickly. A family could fall out of favor just as quickly as it had risen.

Christian Society

During the Byzantine era, Christianity was widely accepted, and the majority of the population converted to it. The clergy formed their own class and played a very important part in society. The Eastern Church was headed by the patriarch of Constantinople. However, the Byzantine emperors also had a measure of control over the church. The emperor was allowed to appoint or remove patriarchs as he saw fit. Beneath the patriarch were local bishops, who took care of smaller regions and reported back to Constantinople.

Stained glass in a Coptic church in Egypt.
someone10x, CC BY 2.0 https://creativecommons.org/licenses/by/2.0 via Wikimedia Commons; https://commons.wikimedia.org/wiki/File:Coptic_church_in_Egypt_(9198216449).jpg

Priests were allowed to marry, but once they became a bishop, they were required to separate from their wives in order to concentrate on their appointment. The wife would then have to retreat to a monastery. Women were allowed to become nuns and dedicate their lives to Christ. Nuns were required to take care of the poor and sickly. Monasteries were communal buildings that often served the needs of the community.

Islamic Society

As Egypt became an increasingly Islamic society, the rules and customs of the country changed once again. During the Arabic caliphates, regions were required to report back to the capital of the empire, and Arabs enjoyed a privileged position in the social hierarchy. However, in time, the caliphates' power dwindled, and smaller regions broke away under opposing caliphates. In Egypt, a person's status depended on their social class, gender, legal status, religion, and ethnicity. While other religions were allowed to coexist among Muslims, at least for the most part, the treatment of non-Muslims varied greatly. Non-Muslims were required to submit to Islamic law and pay a special tax called the jizya, which allowed them to become a part of a protected class called the dhimmi. Unfortunately, the dhimmi didn't enjoy the same social and legal privileges as Muslims.

During the Umayyad Caliphate, non-Arabs were known as mawali and didn't enjoy the same privileges as Arabs. In time, Persians and other non-Arabs were incorporated into the Abbasid state, which allowed the mawali to advance socially. Islamic society was dominated by Islamic laws and traditions, but this also depended on whether a person was a part of the Sunni or Shia branch of Islam. Women were usually allowed to participate in agriculture and develop artisanal skills but were more often relegated to roles that involved homemaking, food preparation, midwifery, and medicine. However, there were different rules that women had to live by according to their religion or socio-economic status. Women were allowed to retain financial and legal independence, which was unusual in other medieval societies. Women were also allowed to invest money, manage their wealth, trade, get divorced, or be included in inheritance (although they often inherited less than their male relatives).

Most cultures dictated that a family would be led by a patriarch. However, some societies, such as the Mamluk society, allowed people more freedom, and women had more independence. During this time, Egyptian society was divided into the urban elite, merchants, landowners, ordinary people (including farmers and artisans), and slaves. When the Mamluks took over, they became the dominant social class.

Ottoman Social Structure

The Ottoman Empire was incredibly large and comprised of different cultures, which means that its social structure had to be complex to accommodate the diversity. Muslim Ottomans generally held more influence than Christians and Jews. The Ottomans also used the millet system, which meant that people of each faith were judged according to their laws. This meant there were different laws for Jews, Christians, and Muslims. Non-Muslims were forced to pay higher taxes, and Christians paid a blood tax (their firstborn sons were taken away, converted to Islam, and forced to serve in the Ottoman army).

The highest social positions were held by people within the sultan's government, which included the sultan's household, the army, bureaucrats, scribes, judges, lawyers, and teachers. The Turks made up the most of this class and were able to rise within the government more easily than others. Meanwhile, the vast majority of the population were laborers, which included farmers and artisans. Conversion wasn't widely promoted; Muslims paid lower taxes, and this would have caused disaster for the Ottoman Empire if everyone had become Muslim.

In Egypt, Cairo became just another provincial city, robbing it of the influence that the Mamluks had lavished on it during their reign. However, the Mamluks continued to be a powerful social class. Unfortunately for Egypt, the Ottomans forced the Europeans to change their trading routes, which meant Egypt became isolated from the rest of the world. Its culture and society remained virtually unchanged for decades.

Life during the British Occupation

When the French invaded Egypt, they interrupted a period of prolonged stagnation of Egyptian culture. They once again opened Egypt to the rest of the world, but that didn't always help the Egyptians. They were forced to live through several violent wars, as well as British interference in their politics. British and French soldiers were stationed in Egypt, while European diplomats and officials moved to Egypt, where they received special treatment.

As a result of European interference, the Egyptian government and economy were destabilized, which led to disastrous consequences for ordinary Egyptians. While foreigners were given special privileges, Egyptians received aid and support from European countries, such as Britain and France, which allowed the Europeans to meddle in Egyptian affairs under the guise of protecting their financial interests. During the 20th century, Egypt had grown tired of European interference, and fierce nationalism swept the nation. This led to riots, uprisings, and revolutions, which further destabilized the country and society. During the British occupation, Egyptians faced martial law, higher taxes, inflation, and forced military conscription. In time, Egypt was able to win its independence, and Egyptian society was allowed to develop naturally.

Chapter 10: The Nile and Its Key Role

The Nile is the longest river in Africa and flows through several countries directly into the Mediterranean Sea. It is the main source of water for Egypt, Sudan, and South Sudan, which makes it a vitally important river that also supports the economies of those countries.

Historically, the Nile River was thought to be the world's longest river, but researchers discovered that the Amazon River is slightly longer. The Nile is comprised of two major tributaries: the White Nile and the Blue Nile. The White Nile flows from Lake Victoria in Uganda, while the Blue Nile begins in Ethiopia. The northern part of the river flows through the Sudanese River directly into Egypt, where it forms a large delta, where Cairo was built. From there, it flows into the Mediterranean Sea, where Alexandria was built.

Thanks to its annual flooding, the plains surrounding the Nile are incredibly fertile, which allowed several civilizations to make their homes on its banks. The river was vitally important to the ancient Egyptians, and that importance is reflected in their religion. For thousands of years, the Nile played a massive role in Egypt's economy and daily life. Later, the search for the source of the Nile would be an enduring mystery that plagued scientists and explorers. Due to its impact on its surroundings, the Nile has a fascinating story to tell.

Foundation of the Egyptian Civilization

Thousands of years ago, North Africa had a much different climate. The region used to experience much more rainfall. However, in time, the lush wetlands dried up and turned into deserts, which forced ancient civilizations to relocate to wetter areas. Thankfully, many of them didn't have to move too far, as the Nile flowed directly through the desert and created fertile plains that were perfect for farming. When the first inhabitants arrived on the banks of the Nile, they discovered that there was plenty of food. They also realized that there was a period of six months when the river rose, then receded, leaving behind a layer of silt. This silt was perfect for farming, and soon, several cultures lived on the banks of the Nile and raised crops.

Once those early cultures discovered irrigation, farming became a regular practice and the basis of many cultures. The Nile provided a regular source of food, and people grew crops such as wheat, cotton, and beans. Since people no longer needed to move around to find food, they were able to establish permanent settlements that eventually turned into cities, which then gave rise to the Egyptian kingdoms. However, the Nile wasn't always regular, which led people to believe that the gods had something to do with the annual flooding. The ancient Egyptians believed that the Nile was a gift from the gods, and much of their culture was structured around the Nile. For instance, their calendar was centered around the Nile, as their year began with the first month of flooding. In an effort to please the gods and ensure regular flooding, the Egyptians developed an intricate religious structure that involved offerings and festivals.

Besides farming, the Nile also allowed the Egyptians to develop skills like boat-making, which later led to them using the Nile as a source of transportation and trade.

Geography

The Nile is about 4,160 miles (around 6,700 kilometers) long and flows northward from east-central Africa to the Mediterranean. It's comprised of tributaries that are fed by smaller rivers, and the flow depends on the arrival of the rainy season. The Blue Nile, one of the most important tributaries, begins from Lake Tana in Ethiopia, where it flows for about 870 miles (about 1,400 kilometers) until it meets up with the White Nile in Khartoum, Sudan. Ethiopia's rainy season usually takes place in the summer, which leads to strong flowing waters that cause erosion and carry highly fertile silt. However, during the dry season, the flow is extremely slow, and in some places, the river dries up completely.

Parts of the Nile Basin can be found in a number of African countries, namely Tanzania, Rwanda, Burundi, the Democratic Republic of the Congo, Uganda, Kenya, South Sudan, Ethiopia, Sudan, and Egypt. The ancient Egyptians used the Nile to make sense of the world around them and divided their region into two important areas. The first part was Kemet, the fertile land of the Nile Valley and surrounding oases. The second part was the Deshret, which was desert lands that didn't have enough resources to sustain people and was, therefore, linked to death and disorder.

Flora and Fauna

Since the Nile runs through such a long stretch of land, there are different regions, and each has a unique environment. The land surrounding the Nile in Egypt was carefully cultivated over thousands of years and provided regular crops of wheat, flax, cotton, papyrus, and barley. These staple crops provided enough grain to feed the Egyptians and allow them to trade with other countries. The Egyptians were also able to grow lentils, peas, watermelons, leeks, and spices, such as cumin and coriander.

The Nile housed many different species of animals. If Egyptians didn't want to be farmers, they could rely on the Nile to provide enough fish to make a living. Fishermen could catch Nile perch, bolti, catfish, tigerfish, or the elephant snout fish. The Nile crocodile, soft-shelled turtle, and hippopotamus were also regular sights for ancient Egyptians. The Nile is home to monitor lizards and around thirty species of snakes, including the infamous asp that may have played a part in Cleopatra's suicide. In less watered areas, flora and fauna are scarcer, and the desert areas around the Nile have fewer forms of life. Some areas have thinly foliaged trees with some grass and herbs.

Irrigation and Farming

Every year, the rains allowed the Nile's water to surge toward Egypt. As it flowed, it carried rich, nutritious soil from the Horn of Africa that was so dark it often looked black. Once the water arrived, the Egyptian farmers were able to begin their farming season. Historians believe the Egyptians were among the earliest farmers who learned to irrigate their lands, although they did so through a process of trial and error. When the Nile flooded, it would cover the land with water, which would destroy homes and fields. While the flooding brought life-giving nutrients, the Egyptians soon realized they would need to find a way to control it. This led ancient Egyptians to dig channels and basins, which would have been a lengthy process.

As the ancient Egyptians developed irrigation, they formed a system called basin irrigation. The farmers would dig networks of land to create basins. From there, they built channels that would funnel the Nile's waters into the basins, where the water would stay and sink into the soil. Once the water evaporated, the land would be ready for planting.

In order to keep track of the Nile's water level, the ancient Egyptians used nilometers, which were basic columns with markings. Nilometers could help Egyptians determine if they were facing unusual flooding. Both too much and too little water would be disastrous. In the 1950s, Gamal Abdel Nasser began the Aswan High Dam building project, which was completed in the 1970s. The Aswan Dam increased the amount of hydroelectric power that could be generated from the Nile and regulated the Nile's flooding. This led to better agricultural practices that benefited Egypt's farmers and economy.

Transportation and Trade

Besides developing agriculture and irrigation, the ancient Egyptians also discovered that they could use the Nile for transportation. In time, Egyptians were able to create wooden boats with sails and oars that could travel great distances. Smaller boats were made of papyrus reeds that had wooden frames. These smaller boats were for small-scale traveling or fishing. As early as the Old Kingdom, Egyptians transported cattle, fish, bread, wood, and vegetables, which were taken to different parts of the kingdom or other kingdoms for trade. Boats quickly became an integral part of Egyptian culture. Kings and important officials were usually buried with their boats, which were perfectly built and could have been used on the Nile.

Ancient mosaic of the Nile.
Ad Meskens, CC BY-SA 3.0 https://creativecommons.org/licenses/by-sa/3.0 via Wikimedia Commons; https://commons.wikimedia.org/wiki/File:Sousse_mosaic_Nile_landscape.JPG

Since Egypt had access to rich agricultural resources, the Egyptians were able to trade their goods with other countries. Not only did this make the kingdom richer, but it also led to peaceful diplomatic ties with their neighbors. Thanks to the Nile, goods could be quickly transported through Egypt. Egypt also occupied an advantageous geographical position that connected it to international trade routes. The empire was connected to Mediterranean trade routes thanks to Alexandria, as well as trade routes with the East because of its position on the Red Sea. Trade was an invaluable part of the Egyptian economy, and Egypt's trade routes developed quickly due to the Nile's extensive waters.

Economy

Agriculture was a massive part of Egypt's economy. Due to Egypt's year-round warm weather and the Nile's regular flooding, Egyptians could sometimes produce as many as three harvests in a year. They produced much more food than they needed, while neighboring Middle Eastern countries often faced droughts and famine, which meant that they sorely needed grain and crops that Egypt could provide. The ancient Egyptians had access to flax, papyrus, stone, and gold, which could be used to make cloth, buildings, jewelry, and paper. As artisans developed their crafts, they were able to create beautiful artworks, such as icons and carvings, which could also be traded for considerable amounts of money. Besides crops, the Nile provided enough water and grazing lands for animals such as cattle and sheep. Oxen were used to plow fields and allowed farmers even quicker yields. Besides labor, animals also produced meat and milk.

Papyrus was another crucial part of Egypt's economy. The plant grew abundantly on the banks of the Nile and could be used to make boats, baskets, and paper. The Egyptians were the first culture to discover how to make paper, and it quickly became Egypt's main export, which caused the Egyptians to conceal the paper-making process so that they could control the paper trade. Egypt also produced massive amounts of gold, wood, iron, silver, and spices. This led to the development of superior weapons and metalwork. Egyptian royalty made sure to benefit by taxing harvests and property. Taxes could be paid with grain, animals, or labor, while merchants had to pay additional taxes. This enriched the pharaoh and the government, allowing them to build public buildings and support the country during times of crisis. Pharaohs were also responsible for opening new avenues of trade, which would have boosted the economy further.

Nilus

The Greeks were fascinated by Egypt and thought that it was a mysterious land filled with wisdom. Eventually, the two cultures merged and were heavily influenced by each other when Alexander the Great conquered Egypt. The Greeks knew that the Nile was the source of life in Egypt, and like the Egyptians, they attributed its abundance to the gods. However, the Greeks didn't share the same beliefs as the Egyptians and developed their own Nile god called Nilus. In fact, the modern word "Nile" comes from the Greek word "Nelios" (another way to spell Nilus), which means river. The ancient Egyptians called the Nile "Ar," which means black. It's as if the Egyptians named the river after the dark sand that was responsible for their nutritious crops.

Nilus was a minor Greek god who didn't have much of an impact on Greek mythology. According to the Greeks, Nilus was the son of the Titans Oceanus and Tethys. Oceanus was the son of Gaea and Chaos, and he married his sister. Together, the Titans had many children called the Oceanids and Potamoi, who were the gods and goddesses of the seas, rivers, and springs. According to Greek mythology, the Titans had so many children that they overproduced and caused floods. In response, the Titans got divorced to prevent flooding the whole Earth with water. Nilus had several children of his own, including Memphis, Europa, and Thebe, among others.

Hapi and Khnum

The Nile was closely associated with ancient Egyptian religion, and most gods and goddesses were involved with the Nile in one way or another. However, according to the ancient Egyptians, there were two main gods who were responsible for the Nile's gifts: Hapi and Khnum. Khnum was the god of fertility, and he was usually involved with procreation and water. He was depicted as a man with a ram's head and often had long, twisting horns. The ancient Egyptians believed that Khnum created humans from clay. This would have resonated with the ancient Egyptians since vast amounts of clay could be found along the banks of the river. The god had several cults, including one at Herwer (his cult's main center). During the New Kingdom, he was associated with the island of Elephantine and thought to be the lord of the First Cataract of the Nile River. He was often associated with the goddesses Satis and Anuket.

Hapi was believed to be the personification of the annual flooding of the Nile. He was also associated with fertility, and he wielded an immense amount of influence in ancient Egypt. Hapi was a somewhat androgynous figure with a large body, a massive belly, and drooping breasts, which would have represented the god's amazing fertility. The god was also depicted as wearing a false beard and a loincloth, which were the garments often worn by workers. Hapi was sometimes depicted as a hippopotamus. While Hapi was closely associated with the Nile, he wasn't considered the god of the Nile but rather the god of the Nile's flooding. He was usually portrayed as a caring father, and his priests carried out rituals that were supposed to ensure the steady flow of the Nile. Hapi's priests also took care of the official nilometer, which they monitored carefully.

The Nile and Egyptian Religion

Besides Khnum and Hapi, the ancient Egyptian religion was intimately connected to the Nile. In fact, the principle of ma'at, which governed Egyptian religion and daily life, may have been influenced by the river. The Nile rose consistently in the middle of July and then fell sometime in September, which may have impressed the importance of harmony and balance to the Egyptians. If the Nile failed to rise or fall on time, it would have disastrous consequences for the Egyptians. Therefore, the Egyptians became keenly aware of what could happen if the world's forces were out of balance, and they were greatly concerned about the order of things staying in balance.

The Egyptians believed that the gods were responsible for the rise and fall of the Nile and that the gods had gifted the Nile to their people. Most of the gods in Egyptian mythology had something to do with the Nile. Sometimes, the gods were directly involved in the Nile's processes or were influenced by the Nile in some way. For example, in the myth of Seth and Osiris, Seth got rid of his brother's body by throwing him into the Nile. In some myths, either Osiris or Isis was responsible for helping the Egyptians discover agriculture and irrigation. The Nile was known as the "Father of Life" and was an extension of Hapi, who was responsible for giving life to the land. It was also known as the "Mother of All Men" since the goddess Ma'at (the godly manifestation of the concepts of harmony and truth) was closely associated with the Nile.

Search for the Source of the Nile

When Europeans began exploring Africa, they quickly discovered the importance and sheer magnitude of the Nile River. This left them with a burning question: what was the source of the Nile? In 1856, an expedition was organized by the Royal Geographical Society. John Hanning Speke and Captain Richard Burton were both accomplished explorers who joined the search. In 1858, they discovered Lake Tanganyika, but Burton was forced to turn back due to illness. Speke continued onward and discovered Lake Victoria, which he correctly claimed was the source of the Nile. Burton didn't agree and thought the source of the Nile was

Lake Tanganyika. The two men would continue to argue about the matter until Speke's death in 1864.

While Lake Victoria is considered to be the source of the Nile, it was discovered that the lake is fed by various tributaries, which made it difficult to locate the "true" source of the Nile. In 2006, explorers claimed that they found the remotest part of the Nile in the Nyungwe Forest near Lake Kivu.

Herodotus, the ancient Greek historian, once wrote that Egypt was the gift of the Nile. It's clear that if it weren't for the Nile, the ancient Egyptians might not have made their permanent home in the Nile Valley. The face of history would have been very different. As scholars delve deeper into the impact of the Nile River on Egypt's history, it becomes clear that if there was no Nile, there would have been no Egypt, or at least not the Egypt that we've come to know.

Chapter 11: The Development of Religion

Religion has always played an important role in Egyptian culture. From its earliest history, an intricate system of worship developed around a pantheon of gods who represented everything from balance to chaos. The ancient Egyptians used religion to relate to the world around them and accredited the gods with everything, both good and bad. They believed that if they kept to the natural harmony by adhering to the strict social hierarchy, contributing to society, and worshiping the gods acceptably, then disasters could be avoided. Whenever disaster struck, the Egyptians believed that it was because the natural balance had been lost.

As Egypt came under foreign rule, its new leaders brought their religions with them. Most foreign empires allowed Egyptians to continue worshiping their traditional religion and had little impact on the Egyptian belief system. When the Greeks took over Egypt, they brought elements of their own religion with them, which led to the formation of new cults. However, when monotheism spread throughout the region, the ancient polytheistic religion began to decline in popularity. Christianity swept through the region, and the new converts rejected the old religion entirely. For years, the

Orthodox Church ruled over Egypt, but it eventually gave way to the spread of Islam, which remains Egypt's national religion today.

Ancient Egyptian Religion

The ancient Egyptians believed that all life was sacred and that nature was controlled by the deities. Their pantheon included both major and minor gods, as well as some humans who had been deified before or after their deaths. In order to avoid disaster, the Egyptians believed they were responsible for angering or appeasing the gods, which meant that religion was involved in every aspect of life, especially in the government. The pharaoh was the head of the religion and the bridge between humans and the gods. As a result, the ancient Egyptians spent enormous amounts of money on rituals, temples, and offerings. While alive, the pharaoh was seen as the son of Ra, a representation of the god Horus. Once he died, the pharaoh was deified and became associated with Ra and Osiris.

The ancient Egyptians also believed in *heka* (magic), which could influence their lives or cause things to happen. Ma'at was also a vital part of the religion, and people believed that ma'at could be renewed. The annual flooding of the Nile was believed to renew ma'at in the universe since it echoed the creation of the universe. Sacred rituals and ceremonies were an important part of Egyptian life, and there were even ceremonies involving names and births. Gods could rise and fall over time, as their cults could gain or lose popularity. In some cases, older gods were replaced by new gods, who then took on the powers or significance of the old god they had replaced.

Egyptian Pantheon

Religion played such an important part in ancient Egyptian culture that the Egyptians worshiped over two thousand gods and goddesses. However, only a few of those gods played major roles in daily life and Egyptian mythology. Some gods became extremely important and became state deities, while others merely represented certain regions or played a specific role in mythology. For example,

Seshat was the goddess of specific measurements and written words. Each god had their own name and specific personality. They were highly individualistic and represented by different clothing, objects, or animals. Some gods changed over time to adopt new personalities or took on a different meaning. For example, the goddess Neith was a war goddess who eventually became a nurturing mother goddess who settled the gods' disputes.

Statue of Horus, Isis, and Osiris.
Metropolitan Museum of Art, CC0, via Wikimedia Commons;
https://commons.wikimedia.org/wiki/File:Isis,_Osiris_and_Horus_triad_MET_23.6.11_00
1.jpg

Some of the most important gods were Isis, Osiris, Horus, Amun, Ra, Hathor, Neith, Sekhmet, Bastet, Thoth, Anubis, Seth, and Ptah. Isis, Osiris, and Horus were frequently depicted in carvings, and their myth dictated the basis of pharaonic authority and the Egyptian afterlife. Hathor was a goddess strongly associated with entertainment; she was the goddess of dancing, drunkenness, and music. She was also the reflection of the Nile River and was originally known as Sekhmet, a destructive goddess who was also associated with Bastet.

Amun or Amun-Ra was another fascinating Egyptian god. At first, he was a minor god, but by the New Kingdom, he was almost exclusively worshiped throughout Egypt and became known as the most powerful of the gods. His priesthood was extremely influential. Specific royal women were appointed as the God's Wife of Amun, which was such a powerful position that it made her almost as powerful as the pharaoh. Sometimes, the Egyptians adopted other gods, such as Anat, the goddess of fertility, sexuality, and war. Anat was originally worshiped in Syria and Canaan but eventually was worshiped in Egypt and became Seth's consort.

The Afterlife

Death was an important part of Egyptian life, as the Egyptians believed their souls lived on after death. This belief caused the Egyptians to build elaborate tombs, craft grave goods (items that were taken with the deceased to the next life), and give offerings to the dead. According to ancient Egyptian mythology, all humans possessed ka, or life essence, which left the body after death. In order to survive in the afterlife, the ka had to consume the life essence of food offerings left by family members. Funeral rites were conducted to release a person's personality so that it could rejoin their ka. Mummification was also an important part of religion, as it was believed that a person's body needed to be kept intact in order to be transported to the afterlife.

Judgment of the dead before Osiris.
*https://commons.wikimedia.org/wiki/File:The_judgement_of_the_dead_in_the_presence_
of_Osiris.jpg*

Once a person's heart was weighed on the scales in front of Osiris, they were either allowed to pass into the afterlife or be devoured by the devourer of souls, Ammit. If a person passed into the afterlife, they were met by a divine ferryman who carried them across Lily Lake into the Field of Reeds. The Field of Reeds was the Egyptian paradise, where everything was like it was on Earth except for sickness, death, and disappointment. However, a person had to pass Osiris's judgment by living a good life in order to enter the Field of Reeds. A lesser goddess known as Amentet met the dead souls as they arrived in the afterlife and provided them with food and drink. Hathor also played a role in the afterlife, as she guided the dead to paradise.

The Cults of Alexander and Serapis

When Ptolemy I began ruling Egypt, he realized that one way to unite the Greeks and Egyptians was through religion. As a result, he created the cults of Alexander and Serapis. The cult of Alexander worshiped the recently deceased Alexander the Great, who was seen as a mighty conqueror and hero. The Egyptians were immensely fond of Alexander, which made it easier for his cult to gain popularity. Ptolemy I constructed a magnificent tomb for Alexander the Great and appointed a priest to perform religious rites at the tomb. This priest became the most important priest in Egypt, and Alexander's tomb became an influential pilgrimage site. Eventually, the Ptolemies associated themselves with the cult, and deceased Ptolemies became gods as well. This enhanced their prestige and firmly established their position over the Egyptians.

Meanwhile, Serapis was a blend of Egyptian and Greek gods, namely Osiris, Apis, and Zeus. This selection was meant to represent the diverse population of Egypt. Serapis had similar powers to Osiris and Apis, which gave him certain transformative abilities, and he had the same authority as Zeus, who was seen as the king of the Greek gods. The cult of Serapis wasn't very popular in Egypt, but it soon spread to Rome and Greece.

Judaism in Egypt

Some of the earliest evidence of Judaism in Egypt can be dated back to around 650 BCE. Around 597 BCE, a large number of Judeans took refuge in Egypt when their governor was assassinated. During the Ptolemaic era, a large number of Jews immigrated to Egypt and settled in Alexandria. By the 3rd century, Jews were living in a number of Egyptian cities and villages and were allowed to exist peacefully in Egypt as they opened businesses and took part in trade. The Ptolemies assigned the Jews a section of the city, as they eventually made up a large number of Alexandria's population. This allowed the Jews to keep their religious practices free from pagan influences. In Alexandria, Jews enjoyed political freedom and lived alongside other religious groups.

In Hellenistic Alexandria, the Jewish community was able to translate the Old Testament into Greek, which came to be known as the Septuagint. However, when Christianity gained popularity in Alexandria during the Byzantine era, the Jews were expelled from the city around 415 CE by Saint Cyril. According to contemporary historians, the Jews were forced to leave the city after a series of controversies and an alleged Jewish-led massacre. During the medieval period, Jews were allowed to live alongside Christians and Muslims, although there were several periods of persecution.

The Spread of Christianity

Christianity began to spread in Egypt in the 1ˢᵗ century CE and quickly became a popular religion, as it appealed to people from all walks of life. It caused the rapid decline of the traditional pagan religion, which had been around for about three thousand years. By the 4ᵗʰ century, Christianity was the most prominent religion in Egypt, and by the 5ᵗʰ century, the Coptic Church had been established. Traditionally, the spread of Christianity in Egypt has been accredited to Saint Mark, but he may have been helped by the missionary Apollos. The Coptic Church had a definite impact on Egyptian culture and art. While Egypt had been conquered by other foreign powers, those empires didn't have much of an impact on Egyptian culture, but Christianity was embraced by the Egyptians, changing many aspects of Egyptian life.

Egypt also played a massive role in the worldwide spread of Christianity. Egypt had a diverse population and received visitors from all over the world due to its intellectual community. The bishops of Egypt played a leading role in developing Christian doctrine, and soon, the religion was influenced by Egyptian beliefs and practices. Monasteries replaced temples and priesthoods as the focal point of daily Egyptian life. However, Christians weren't always left in peace. The Romans allowed conquered lands to keep their religions as long as they recognized the Roman emperor as one of their gods, which the Christians refused to do. This often put them at odds with the Roman Empire, as their refusal to worship the Roman emperor was seen as an act of defiance. During the early years of Christianity, most of the known world was more familiar with polytheism, which made it hard for others to understand the concept of exclusive devotion to one supreme ruler.

Diocletian's Persecution of Christians

Diocletian was the Roman emperor who ruled from 286 to 305 CE. He hoped to reach a compromise with the Christians and declared that he was the son of Jupiter (the king of the Roman gods) and that he was Jupiter's apostle on Earth. This story was likely concocted in an effort to align himself with Christian beliefs, especially with regard to the significance of God's son, Jesus Christ. However, the Christians refused to accept Diocletian's new status and rejected his compromise. While Diocletian was an adept ruler, he was egotistical and took this refusal as an insult. As a result, Diocletian began persecuting Christians throughout the Roman Empire.

The Egyptian Church called this age of persecution the Age of Martyrs due to the number of Christians who were brutally martyred and killed. Thousands were tortured by Roman legions before being murdered, and churches were destroyed, looted, and burned to the ground. Diocletian expected these new acts to force Christianity into extinction. Instead, the persecution only strengthened the zeal of the Christians, and larger numbers began converting to the religion. The early Christians were forced into Roman temples, where they were supposed to worship the statues of Roman gods.

Despite the threat of severe punishment, Christians clung to their beliefs. At first, this surprised Diocletian, but eventually, their defiance enraged him, which led to more atrocities. It was a bloody and violent time for the Romans, but eventually, support for the persecution waned. When Diocletian retired in 305 CE, his persecution ended too. Christians were allowed worship in peace, as Diocletian was the last Roman emperor to severely persecute the Christians. In 306 CE, Constantine became emperor of the Byzantine Empire, and he converted to Christianity. Eventually, Christianity became the Byzantine national religion.

The Spread of Islam

Following the death of Prophet Muhammad, the caliphates were created. They quickly began conquering territories and took the message of their religion with them, which caused Islam to spread to the newly acquired territories. As soon as areas converted, the army was joined by new recruits who were zealous to support the cause. Islam was able to spread quickly because its army kept growing, and eventually, the Islamic Empire grew to hold a significant amount of territory. The most significant time of expansion took place during the Rashidun Caliphate in around 632 CE. During the Rashidun Caliphate, Egypt was conquered and brought under the caliphate's authority, which ruled over Egypt for hundreds of years.

The Rashidun Caliphate based its rule on Islamic principles and brought Muslim economics and trading with them. They were responsible for starting the Islamic Golden Age and introducing a new era of gunpowder warfare. By the 7th century, many Egyptians had converted to Islam, replacing Christianity as the state religion. The Islamic world was diverse and led to the creation of centers of culture and science. Trade also boomed, as the Muslim world traded resources and developed diplomatic relationships based on their religion. Several dynasties rose to dominance, but the massive ruling caliphate was soon replaced by smaller, regional caliphates, such as the Fatimid Caliphate in Egypt. This change had massive consequences for Egypt, as the former ruling caliphs belonged to the Sunni branch of Islam, while the Fatimids belonged to the Shia branch of Islam.

Islam during the Fatimid Caliphate

The Shia and Sunni branches of Islam share many similarities; for instance, they all accept the importance of the Quran, they both draw from the Hadith, and they accept the five pillars of Islam. However, their main differences center around the question of religious authority, and their split occurred shortly after the death of Prophet Muhammad. When the prophet died, there were serious questions about who would be his successor. Some preferred his cousin, Ali, and they later formed the Shia branch of Islam. Meanwhile, the Sunni followed the prophet's closest friend, Abu Bakr. The Sunni base their worship on the example of Prophet Muhammad, while the Shia focus on Muhammad's successors in the form of imams (religious instructors), who are thought to be divinely appointed.

The Fatimids were firmly Shia Muslims and were determined to bring an end to the Abbasid Caliphate, as they hoped to become the rulers of the Muslim world. This would allow them to impose their belief system on other Muslims and finally settle the matter of Prophet Muhammad's succession. Despite this goal, the Fatimids are known for being remarkably tolerant toward all religions. They allowed Christians, Jews, and Sunni Muslims to advance within the government and valued certain women's rights. The Fatimids used Egypt as their base and promoted religious scholarship and Egypt's economy. Their rule was a time of cultural enlightenment and advancement in Egypt. However, many of their policies were reversed by Saladin when he conquered the region.

Modern Egyptian Religion

The Egyptian state religion is still Islam, and the country remains firmly embedded in the Muslim world. The population is primarily made up of Sunni Muslims who follow the Maliki school of thought. However, the state is also comprised of Shia Muslims, Christians, and Jews, who together make up about 10 percent of the population. Egypt remains a diverse country with a wide array of Islamic views. There are sporadic reports of religious intolerance, but this is true in most countries.

Chapter 12: Language, Art, and Architecture

As soon as the Egyptian civilization developed, its culture grew along with its population. The ancients found ways to make sense of the world around them, which influenced everything from their beliefs to their architecture. Ancient Egyptian culture was so strong that we still see echoes of it thousands of years later. By taking a look at the fascinating art, architecture, and literature left behind by the ancient Egyptians, we can gain a unique perspective on their lives. Thousands of artifacts were left behind in sealed tombs, which provide scholars with ample evidence of what the Egyptian culture looked like before it was influenced by foreign conquerors.

When powerful empires invaded and took over Egypt, they left their mark on Egyptian culture. While some foreign rulers allowed the Egyptian culture to stagnate, others took a keen interest in the land of pharaohs and made valuable contributions to Egypt's language and art.

Hieroglyphics

The first evidence of hieroglyphic script can be traced back to around 3100 BCE, just as Egypt developed its unique pyramid-like social structure. While the script uses pictures, the pictures don't always mean what they represent. Rather, hieroglyphs depict certain sounds in the ancient Egyptian language, just as the characters in modern alphabets represent sounds. Hieroglyphs were first used in royal tombs to leave a record of the king's life and deeds. In time, other Egyptians began using hieroglyphs, but hieroglyphs remained the primary script for royal tombs and monuments. While hieroglyphs are intimately associated with Egyptian culture, most Egyptians didn't use hieroglyphs or understand what they meant. Since hieroglyphs were difficult to create, the Egyptians developed hieratic writing, which was a type of cursive script. Later, demotic writing was developed for ordinary documents.

Egyptian hieroglyphs.
Hosni bin Park, CC BY-SA 4.0 https://creativecommons.org/licenses/by-sa/4.0 via Wikimedia Commons; https://commons.wikimedia.org/wiki/File:Egyptian_hieroglyphics.jpg

In ancient Egypt, hieroglyphs weren't common among the lower classes, which meant that only priests were able to read them. Ordinary people were taught demotic instead. In time, hieroglyphs died out as the pharaohs were replaced by foreign rulers. The Ptolemies made Greek the official court language, and in 384 CE, the Roman emperor outlawed the Egyptian pagan religion, which caused hieroglyphs to die out. The Rosetta Stone eventually allowed historians to decipher hieroglyphics, but it's still a tricky endeavor.

The Egyptian verbal system was never fully written out, and hieroglyphics contain many quirks, which makes them difficult to translate. The translation of hieroglyphs can also be subjective, which has led to a lot of confusion in the scholarly community.

Ancient Egyptian Tombs

The Egyptians were extremely concerned about preserving their bodies after death and ensuring they had a successful transition from the living world to the afterlife. As a result, the first kings of Egypt began building elaborate tombs, which were filled with everything they felt they needed in the afterlife. The first of these tombs were called mastabas. These tombs usually had inscriptions with the king's name. The mastabas were cut into rocky outcrops and featured sunbaked bricks and wooden boards. It's possible that when a king died, a large number of servants were sacrificed so they could serve the king in his afterlife. This practice is evidenced by a large number of graves containing women and dwarves that have been found around the mastabas. The royal tombs were also filled with jars, furniture, and various offerings that were buried with the king so that he could maintain his luxurious lifestyle in the afterlife.

Eventually, royal tombs and monuments became more elaborate, which led to the construction of large pyramids. However, grave robbing became prevalent, which was a serious concern for the royal family. If their tombs were plundered, they would be stranded in the afterlife without all their riches. As a result, the royals of the New Kingdom chose a new remote location for their tombs, which became known as the Valley of the Kings.

The Pyramids of Giza

The Egyptian rulers had good reason to worry about their afterlife. They believed they would be gods and rulers in the next life, which meant they had to prepare their tombs with everything they would need to be good leaders. As a result, the construction of royal tombs was a matter of national importance. Pharaoh Khufu was the first king to build his pyramid at Giza, beginning the project around 2550 BCE. The pyramid is a magnificent building made up of about 2.3 million stone blocks and stands at about 481 feet (147 meters). Khufu's pyramid is the biggest as well. Khafre, Khufu's successor, followed his father's example and built his pyramid at Giza too. He may also have been responsible for the Sphinx, which watches over the grand complex. Finally, the last pyramid at Giza was built by Menkaure around 2490 BCE. While Menkaure's pyramid isn't as big as the others, it has an intricate mortuary complex.

The Pyramids of Giza
Walkerssk, CC0, via Wikimedia Commons;
https://commons.wikimedia.org/wiki/File:Pyramids_in_Giza_-_Egypt.jpg

The pyramids were meant to be more than just tombs and were built on a massive complex that featured temples and palaces. Since the pyramids were a matter of national importance, ordinary Egyptians contributed to the projects. Historians have found evidence of a temporary city that showed the workers of the pyramids were generally happy and well-fed. It also seems that skilled workers volunteered to be part of the pharaohs' projects.

The Temple at Saqqara

The temple complex at Saqqara may be one of Egypt's most famous and important archaeological sites. Saqqara is south of Cairo and is marked by the Step Pyramid, which was built by Djoser during the Old Kingdom. The Step Pyramid is also the oldest known stone building complex in history. There are several other important pyramids and tombs at the site, which is about five miles long. Historians have found thousands of artifacts at the site, which give them an invaluable glimpse into ancient Egyptian life. The necropolis has also revealed "mega-tombs," which contained hundreds of coffins, mummies, and mummified cats. Burial goods, such as portrait masks, gems, and artworks, have also been uncovered at Saqqara.

The site has a large number of underground caverns, which were used for burials but have been looted as time passed. Saqqara first attracted scholarly attention around 1850 when it was discovered by Auguste Mariette, a French Egyptologist. According to his report, the site had been looted, as he found mummy wrappings lying in the sand. He was the first to note the significance of the sphinx-lined street that led to the Serapeum, an important temple at Saqqara. The temple was also the burial place of the Apis cult's bulls, which represented the gods Osiris and Ptah. For three thousand years, Saqqara served as the site of important non-royal burials and religious ceremonies. It became a UNESCO World Heritage Site in 1979.

The Great Sphinx in Gaza

The Great Sphinx is one of Egypt's most famous and recognizable monuments. Sphinxes were mythological creatures with the body of a lion and the head of a human. The Great Sphinx was cut from limestone and stands at about 66 feet (20 meters) high and is 240 feet (73 meters) long. The face of the Sphinx seems to represent Pharaoh Khafre, but its nose was broken off sometime between the 3rd and 10th century CE. Despite the mystery of what happened to its nose, the Great Sphinx is known as the oldest monumental sculpture in Egypt and is certainly a unique piece of architecture that has endured for thousands of years.

The Great Sphinx.
Hamerani, CC BY-SA 4.0 https://creativecommons.org/licenses/by-sa/4.0 via Wikimedia Commons; https://commons.wikimedia.org/wiki/File:Great_Sphinx_of_Giza_(2).jpg

The construction of the Great Sphinx has been a source of fascination and mystery for hundreds of years. It appears that the Sphinx was made from the same stones that were used to build the pyramids and may have originated from the same quarry. Some historians have suggested that the head was carved first out of a large rock that had already been shaped by the wind. The Sphinx's body was made out of the same stones that were used to build the temple that stands in front of it. Strangely, the temple was never completed, and there's no evidence that there was ever a sphinx cult in Egypt. It's possible that Khafre built the Great Sphinx in order to protect the Saqqara complex, which was an important site in ancient Egypt.

Fortresses

Egypt was an extremely fertile and profitable region, which meant that it attracted the attention of neighboring countries that would have seen the value of invading the country and adding its riches to their own nation. As a result, the pharaohs of Egypt had to be constantly on guard. In order to keep their nation safe, the pharaohs built fortresses, border posts, and walls to protect areas that were vulnerable to attack. Most pharaohs concentrated on defending the territories they already had, which means that for most of Egypt's history, it didn't have a standing army. The ancient Egyptians spent a lot of time and effort building and maintaining border fortresses that kept them safe from the threat of invasion.

One of the most important fortresses was built between the Second and First Cataracts of the Nile and was called Buhen. It served as an Egyptian outpost as early as around 2770 BCE and became an important fortress during the New Kingdom. The complex was made up of massive outer walls, interior temples, and bastions, which were common features of ancient Egyptian fortresses. Buhen was made out of rocks and bricks and was built along the river and a rocky slope. In order to prevent invaders from scaling it, a steep ditch was carved into the rock. Hatshepsut built a temple in the southern part of Buhen, and later pharaohs either renovated the site or added their own shrines.

Ramesses II, or Ramesses the Great, was also known for building extensively, and he built a number of fortresses along Egypt's northwestern coast.

New Kingdom Temples and Tombs

The New Kingdom was known as Egypt's golden age. As Egypt gained more influence and wealth due to its foreign conquests, the pharaohs were able to build on a much larger and grander scale than ever before. Hatshepsut, in particular, was known for building incredible structures that were unlike anything that had been built in Egypt before. The Temple of Hatshepsut was the queen's mortuary temple and features a stunning colonnaded structure that predates the Parthenon. It was built into a cliff face and houses a series of terraces that were once filled with cultivated gardens.

Ramesses II was another great builder. He constructed the Tomb of Nefertari in the Valley of the Kings, as well as the Ramesseum. The Tomb of Nefertari features stunning wall paintings, and the Ramesseum features enormous carvings that depict highlights from the king's reign.

Luxor Temple.
© *Vyacheslav Argenberg http://www.vascoplanet.com , CC BY 4.0*
https://creativecommons.org/licenses/by/4.0 via Wikimedia Commons;
https://commons.wikimedia.org/wiki/File:Luxor_Temple,_Luxor,_Egypt.jpg

Important New Kingdom temples include the Luxor Temple. This complex was built near the ancient city of Thebes and featured six massive temples. The temples contain many examples of illusionism and symbolism, which were prevalent in ancient Egyptian architecture. For example, two obelisks were built to emphasize a pathway and give the illusion that they're the same height even though they aren't. The temples at Karnak are another important ancient site. They were used to worship the god Amun, whose priesthood wielded incredible influence in Egypt. The complex is now the biggest ancient religious site in the world and a popular museum.

Copts

The Copts are Egypt's largest indigenous Christian community and have existed in Egypt ever since the original spread of Christianity. The Coptic Orthodox Church remains the largest

Christian church in Egypt. Before the spread of Islam, Egyptians spoke a form of language called Coptic. However, Muslim Egyptians eventually stopped using Coptic, and it came to identify the Christian minority. The Coptic dialect family descended from the ancient Egyptian language and emerged around the 3rd century CE. It quickly became the most popular language in Egypt, as it spread throughout the country along with Christianity. The language bore many Greek influences and was written using the Coptic alphabet, which was a mixture of the Greek and demotic scripts.

Some of the oldest Coptic scripts predate the Christian era and are written in Old Coptic. However, most Coptic literature features texts that were written by members of the Coptic Church, who later became saints. Shenoute was a saint known for popularizing and improving Coptic through his homilies, sermons, and treatises, which make up a large portion of early Coptic literature. For several centuries, Christianity was Egypt's main religion, and it had a massive influence on Egyptian art and led to distinct buildings and artworks.

Coptic Art and Architecture

When Roman Emperor Theodosius outlawed pagan religions, Christianity became the national Egyptian religion. Egypt was forever changed. The Coptic Christians often transformed existing ancient temples, tombs, and shrines into monasteries, churches, and martyrs' shrines. Christians from all over the Byzantine Empire visited the significant holy sites associated with the saints, and the Bible was translated into Coptic, which led to the development of original Egyptian Christian literature. Coptic churches were lavishly decorated with colorful murals, natural motifs, and inscriptions of Bible extracts, psalms, and monastic accounts. Gravestones were often decorated with crosses, doves, and foliage patterns.

Saint Mark's Coptic Orthodox Cathedral, Egypt.

Floral and faunal motifs became popular themes in Coptic architecture, as they often represented paradise. Pottery also bore similar markings and featured inscriptions from the Bible. The Copts built great cathedrals, such as Saint Mark's Coptic Orthodox Cathedral. Monasteries also became popular, and many ancient monasteries, such as the Monastery of Saint Anthony, still exist in Egypt. Some Coptic cathedrals shared similar floor plans and architectural elements with earlier temples. For example, some churches had a hidden inner sanctuary, which was a common feature in Egyptian temples. However, Coptic churches were eventually influenced by Byzantine architecture. As the centuries progressed, Coptic buildings began to show evidence of Islamic influence.

Arabic

When the Rashidun Caliphate arrived in Egypt in the 7th century, Coptic was the national Egyptian language, although Greek was still used for administrative matters. While Coptic and Greek were widely used, they were still relatively new languages. Greek had been introduced as a state language by the Ptolemies but was mainly used by statesmen and foreign merchants. Christianity gained traction in Egypt around the 4th and 5th centuries, which caused a massive shift from classical Greek practices and religion. By 451 CE, there was a massive divide between the Egyptian and Greek churches, which put an even greater distance between the Egyptians and Greeks. While Coptic was the main literary language in Egypt, it was still a relatively new language since it was a unique blend of Greek and ancient Egyptian.

Coptic remained popular in Egypt even under Arabic rule, as it was the sole language of the church. For the first century or so of Arabic rule, Arabic was still reserved for Arab immigrants, government officials, and the ruling elite. Eventually, a large number of Arabs moved to Egypt, and the Islamic rulers were forced to defeat a Coptic peasant revolt. In time, many Egyptians converted to Islam, and the Copts were forced to pay excessive tax rates. By the 8th and 9th centuries, most Egyptians were speaking Arabic, and it became the primary language in the country. In modern times, the national language of Egypt is Modern Standard Arabic, which is a standardized literary version of Arabic. It was developed during the 19th and 20th centuries and conformed to a written standard.

Islamic Art and Architecture

During early Islamic rule in Egypt, Cairo became the center of administration and religion. As a result, it became home to some of the most magnificent examples of Islamic architecture in the world. Islamic art is intricately tied to the religion and usually represents the principle of divine unity. Calligraphy is extremely popular, as it is used to write out portions of the Quran. Mosques are probably the first thing that comes to people's minds when they think of Islamic architecture. Over time, Egypt's architecture began bearing Ayyubid, Fatimid, Mamluk, Ottoman, and other modern styles, which reflected the styles of each ruling class and their periods.

The Mosque of Ibn Tulun.

One of the most stunning examples of Islamic architecture in Cairo is the Mosque of Ibn Tulun. Ibn Tulun set up a ruling dynasty in Egypt after he was sent there to serve as a governor in Fustat. The mosque was built to resemble the great mosque in Samarra, Iraq, which was Ibn Tulun's childhood home. It also featured elements of Spanish architecture. Egypt is also home to the ancient Mosque of Amr ibn al-As, which was built just a few years after the death of Prophet Muhammad and shortly after the Islamic conquest of Egypt. The Mosque of Amr ibn al-As was the oldest mosque in Africa; it has been rebuilt several times over the centuries.

Besides mosques, madrasas and minarets came to dominate the Egyptian skyline. In fact, Cairo has so many minarets that the city is known as "the City of a Thousand Minarets."

PART FOUR: Key Figures in Egyptian History

Chapter 13: Tutankhamun and his Cursed Tomb (1341–1327 BC)

King Tutankhamun is one of the most famous Egyptian rulers of all time. Unlike many of his predecessors, he isn't famous for his mighty military conquests or prosperous reign; rather, he is widely recognized because of his tomb. When Tutankhamun was still a young boy, he inherited a country that had been plunged into chaos because of his father's fanaticism. The boy king worked with experienced advisors to correct the nation's course. However, those advisors had their own agendas, which would soon become evident when Tutankhamun died. In keeping with the traditions of Egyptian monarchs, Tutankhamun was mummified and placed in a tomb full of riches. Unfortunately, he was placed in a makeshift tomb that was a far cry from the tombs of his predecessors.

Tutankhamun was forgotten by history, as he was replaced by his vizier, Ay, and later by General Horemheb. It wasn't until a British Egyptologist named Howard Carter uncovered the king's tomb in 1922 that Tutankhamun's story was revealed to the world. His tomb was filled with incredible archaeological discoveries, but it soon became the center of rumors and controversy as a supposed curse ripped through Howard Carter's team. Over the next few decades, Tutankhamun's story would fascinate the world as his tomb revealed the secrets of ancient Egyptian politics. Experts have also worked to find the truth behind the fatal "curse."

Tutankhamun's Parents

Akhenaten was a pharaoh during the Eighteenth Dynasty of the New Kingdom. He was the son of the great king Amenhotep III and his wife, Tiye. At first, Akhenaten was known as Amenhotep IV, but he later changed his name to Akhenaten in order to show honor to the god Aten. He was also the husband of the legendary queen Nefertiti, who was known for her capabilities as a ruler and her beauty. During the last years of Amenhotep III's reign, his son ruled as co-regent in order to learn the intricacies of ruling Egypt.

Akhenaten and his family worshiping Aten

However, soon after Akhenaten converted to monotheism, he lost interest in ruling and became obsessed with Aten's religious cult. This meant that his advisors and main wife, Nefertiti, had to pick up the slack and were forced to rule on his behalf. There is some evidence that he occasionally participated in state affairs, but for the most part, he neglected Egypt. Akhenaten was known as a family man and may have had seven or eight children by different wives. Records show that toward the end of his reign, Akhenaten was ruling with a co-regent, possibly his wife Nefertiti or his daughter, Meritaten.

There was some dispute about Tutankhamun's mother, as some thought that Nefertiti was his mother while others believed that his mother was Meketaten, the daughter of Akhenaten and Nefertiti. However, all those claims were proved false when three female mummies were discovered in Amenhotep II's tomb. DNA testing showed that one of the mummies, nicknamed "the Younger Lady," was Akhenaten's sister and Tutankhamun's mother. In 2013, an Egyptologist named Marc Gabolde challenged that theory. He claimed that further DNA testing proved that the Younger Lady was Nefertiti's daughter. In time, historians may find Nefertiti's body and prove that she was Tutankhamun's true mother.

Early Life

As with most monarchies, the Egyptians were very careful when it came to the line of succession. Toward the end of Akhenaten's life, it seems that his duties had been assumed by either one or two co-regents. Not much is known about these co-regents, and their names only appear on a few monuments in Akhetaten that have been dated to the very end of Akhenaten's reign. The inscription refers to Smenkhkare, who shared the coronation name Ankhkheperure with an individual called Neferneferuaten. In ancient Egypt, coronation names were unique to one ruler and weren't shared. This has led many to believe that Smenkhkare may have really been Neferneferuaten (Nefertiti's full name). It's clear that a co-regent was appointed during the last years of Akhenaten's reign. The co-regent ruled for a short period after Akhenaten's death since Tutankhamun was only a child at the time.

Carving of Tutankhamun
https://commons.wikimedia.org/wiki/File:Tutankhamun_tomb_photographs_4_326.jpg

Some historians believe that Smenkhkare may have been Akhenaten's oldest daughter, Meritaten. It isn't clear if she was elevated to this position through marriage to her father or if she was simply given the position. Still, some suggest that Smenkhkare may have been Meritaten's husband. A few scholars have theorized that Smenkhkare could have been one of Akhenaten's sons and that Smenkhkare and Tutankhamun were brothers. The evidence of co-regents suggests that attempts were made to hold the throne until Tutankhamun was old enough to rule. Since not much is known about Smenkhkare, it isn't known how the co-regent's rule ended, but shortly after Akhenaten's death, nine-year-old Tutankhamun became king.

Reign

Tutankhamun inherited the throne around 1333 BCE and promptly married his sister, Ankhesenamun, who was probably his oldest surviving sister. He took on the coronation name of Nebkheperure. Due to his age, he ruled alongside two advisors, Ay and Horemheb. Ay was an accomplished courtier who had long held close ties to the royal family, while Horemheb was a capable military man who had proven himself on the field of battle. Tutankhamun had been named Tutankhaten at birth, but after three years of ruling, he named himself Tutankhamun and moved the royal capital from Akhetaten back to Memphis. It was a decisive move that separated his reign from his father's. Tutankhamun restored the old gods and began restoring the cult of Amun.

During his reign, he also built a temple in Thebes, a palace at Karnak, and added the Colonnade of the Temple of Luxor. Unfortunately, the temple and Karnak were destroyed sometime after his reign. Tutankhamun and Ankhesenamun had two daughters, but the children were stillborn and may have died as a result of complications caused by incest. While Tutankhamun only ruled for about nine years, it's clear that he put a lot of effort into reversing his father's religious policies.

Death

Since Tutankhamun became more famous after his tomb was found, it's only natural that people would be fascinated by the cause of his death. Historians don't agree about what may have killed the king, which has led to the development of several theories. It has been discovered that Tutankhamun was relatively tall but suffered from a terrible bone disease that resulted in a club foot. He probably wasn't a strong child and may have been sickly. Surprisingly, scholars found a hole in the back of his skull, which led many to believe that the young king had been assassinated. This theory was overturned recently when it was revealed that the hole was likely made during the mummification process.

Tests have shown that the king's left leg was broken and infected. The king had multiple malaria infections, all of which could have killed him. CT scans revealed that the young king had a curved spine, a long head, and a cleft palate. His upper vertebrae were fused, which may have made the king's life difficult. Some scholars have theorized that Tutankhamun was involved in a chariot crash that left his legs and pelvis broken. He then contracted an infection that poisoned his blood and killed him.

Unfortunately, experts are unable to tell which of Tutankhamun's bones were broken during his life and what damage was caused by Howard Carter's team. Tutankhamun was buried with several necklaces and rings, which were all removed by Carter's team. The removal process damaged the fragile mummy, which has made identifying his cause of death extremely difficult. It's possible that scholars may never discover what killed the young king, but they certainly won't stop trying to find out.

The Race to Bury King Tutankhamun

While it's not clear why Tutankhamun died, it is clear that he died suddenly and without warning. The line of succession was hazy, and it seems that Horemheb may have been Tutankhamun's accepted successor since he may have had the title of "Crown Prince." Historians theorize that Horemheb had been appointed as Tutankhamun's heir in case the king died without one. As soon as Tutankhamun died, the Egyptian court was plunged into turmoil. Horemheb was in Asia with the Egyptian army and turned back to Egypt as soon as he heard the news, but he would only be able to return after a few months. Ay was still at court and set his sights on becoming king. In order to do that, he would have to be the one to bury the young pharaoh. Ay also had to deal with an unexpected challenge.

Tutankhamun burial chamber.
Romagy, CC BY-SA 4.0 https://creativecommons.org/licenses/by-sa/4.0 via Wikimedia Commons; https://commons.wikimedia.org/wiki/File:Tutankhamun_KV62_burial_chamber_and_sarcophagus.jpg

Tutankhamun's widow, Ankhesenamun, quickly established herself as a contender for the throne, as she may have petitioned the Hittite king to allow her to marry his son. Hittite records indicate that the Hittites received an urgent letter from an Egyptian queen named Nibkhururiya. She begged the Hittite king to send her one of his sons so that she could marry him. The Hittites sent an emissary who returned with another urgent plea and several assurances. If Ankhesenamun truly intended to become queen of Egypt in her own right, her plan would have been abominable to the Egyptians, as it would have been a breach of ma'at to have a foreign king on the throne. The Hittite prince never arrived in Egypt, and it's possible that he was murdered by Ay. There is also evidence that Nefertiti may have been the queen who begged the Hittites for a husband.

While the royal family and courtiers squabbled for dominance, the matter of Tutankhamun's tomb had to be solved. Since the king died before his official tomb was completed, a private tomb was found in the Valley of the Kings and quickly converted. It would appear as though some of Tutankhamun's burial gifts were rushed, and his mummification process may also have been sped up since his skull was likely damaged shortly after his death. In time, the location of Tutankhamun's tomb was lost, and workmen's huts were built over the entrance.

Successors

According to ancient records, it appears that Ay served Akhenaten in Akhetaten as one of his courtiers. Ay likely began his civil service in the military and eventually became the master of the horse and troop leader. Sometime during his career, he became an exceptionally close friend to the royal family. His wife, Tey, also became one of Nefertiti's nurses. It has been suggested that Ay and Tey were Nefertiti's parents, although that claim would be difficult to prove. As soon as Akhenaten died, Ay became one of Tutankhamun's closest advisors and may have led the young king to reverse many of Akhenaten's policies.

Soon after Tutankhamun died, Ay became the king of Egypt, doing so around 1323 BCE. He may have taken the young king's tomb and mortuary temple for himself, as his tomb was much more luxurious than Tutankhamun's. Scholars have found several artifacts bearing the names of Ay and Ankhesenamun, which have led some to believe that Ay married Tutankhamun's widow, but there isn't much evidence to support that fact. While Ay won the throne, he died around 1319 BCE, leaving the throne to Horemheb.

Once Horemheb became king, he continued restoring the temples and cults of the old gods but also began erasing the names of his predecessors, namely, Ay, Tutankhamun, and Akhenaten. He carved his names over their monuments and combined the records of their reigns with his own reign. It's surprising that Horemheb chose to erase his predecessors from history since he was married to Mutnodjmet, who was likely related to the royal family. His marriage and relationship with Tutankhamun suggest that he was close to the royal family. Horemheb would be the last king of the Eighteenth Dynasty and was succeeded by his vizier, Ramesses I.

Howard Carter

Howard Carter was born on May 9th, 1874, in Swaffham, Norfolk, England. He was one of eleven children and showed great artistic talent, which prompted one of the family's neighbors, Lady Amherst, to arrange for Carter to go to Egypt. When he was seventeen years old, he participated in an archaeological survey of Egypt. While working on the survey, he proved his talent by adeptly copying tomb decorations. He later became the inspector general of the Egyptian antiquities department. In 1902, he helped discover the tombs of Hatshepsut and Thutmose IV. Carter kept a diary during his life, which provides an in-depth view of the excavations he oversaw and his discoveries.

During Carter's time as the inspector general, he oversaw numerous excavations and restorations in the Valley of the Kings. In 1904, he was transferred to Lower Egypt, where he was allowed to lead his own excavations. However, he resigned a year later after Egyptian site guards were involved in an altercation with French tourists. He chose to support the Egyptian guards and refused to apologize to the French. In 1907, he was tasked with supervising more excavations in the Valley of the Kings after he was sought out by the 5th Earl of Carnarvon.

Discovery of Tutankhamun's Tomb

Carter and Lord Carnarvon worked together for several seasons but were forced to take a break during World War I. As soon as they were able, they began excavations in the Valley of the Kings. The men soon found several pieces of evidence bearing Tutankhamun's name, which caused Carter to believe they were close to finding the king's tomb. Unfortunately, after years of searching, Carter only found ancient workmen's huts and a few calcite jars. Lord Carnarvon began to lose interest in Carter's theories, but Carter managed to convince the earl to support him for one more season.

Howard Carter examines Tutankhamun's sarcophagus.
https://commons.wikimedia.org/wiki/File:Tuts_Tomb_Opened.JPG

Carter's final season began on November 1ˢᵗ, 1922. He decided to excavate the workmen's huts, and by the time they were done exposing them, they found a step had been carved into the ground. The workers soon revealed a staircase that ended in a covered entrance that bore the seals of the royal necropolis. Later, Carnarvon arrived in Luxor, and the team was able to begin excavations on the tomb. It quickly became apparent that the tomb had been robbed twice after Tutankhamun had been buried, but the tomb had been resealed, which led the team to believe there was still something left. According to Carter's diary, he made a small hole in the tomb's entrance and conducted a few tests to make sure the air in the tomb was safe. Once he determined that it was, he peered into the hole and saw that the tomb was full of "wonderful things."

Contents of the Tomb

Tutankhamun's tomb was much smaller than those of other pharaohs, but due to its small size and obscure location, it was protected from grave robbers. While the entrance hall was plundered soon after his death, the tomb's inner chambers remained untouched. Carter's team found about 5,000 artifacts in the tomb, which included clothes, 130 walking sticks, chariots, furniture, and artwork. There were so many artifacts in the tomb that it took Carter and his team about a decade to fully document their findings.

Tutankhamun tomb photographs.
https://commons.wikimedia.org/wiki/File:Tutankhamun_tomb_photographs_2_026.jpg

One of the most astounding finds was the king's sarcophagus, which was made up of three coffins that all fit into each other. King Tut's coffin was made out of solid gold and still held his body. He was buried with golden statues and jewelry. While the treasures were astounding and certainly valuable, the archaeologists were extremely excited by the discovery of Tutankhamun's mummy. The tomb also contained an unusual dagger with a blade likely made from a meteorite. The objects of the tomb provided a rare glimpse into the lives of the pharaohs and allowed historians a closer glimpse into ancient Egyptian metalworking processes. Tutankhamun's grave goods also revealed the rushed nature of his burial since many of the items were originally meant for other recipients, namely Smenkhkare and Neferneferuaten.

Tutankhamun's Curse

Carter's discovery was impressive because most archaeologists believed that all the tombs in the Valley of the Kings had been completely plundered by grave robbers. When his discovery was announced, the news swept the world, and it became a sensational story. Tourists and reporters streamed to the tomb, and every time something was taken from the tomb, hundreds of cameras went off. During the initial months of the excavation, the tomb was the site of a media circus. As the news spread throughout the world, rumors of a curse were also reported.

Tourists and reporters outside Tutankhamun's tomb.
*https://commons.wikimedia.org/wiki/File:Tourists_outside_Tutankhamun%27s_tomb,_Fe
bruary_1923.jpg*

Several magazines and newspapers reported that "the most dire punishment follows any rash intruder into a sealed tomb." Shortly afterward, Lord Carnarvon died in Cairo, and the city experienced a blackout. This spurred more rumors, and Arthur Conan Doyle joined the fray by telling the press that an evil spirit had been created by the ancient Egyptian priests in order to protect the king. In the following years, the story was perpetuated when several notable people connected to the tomb's discovery died due to mysterious or violent causes. In 1923, Prince Ali Kamel Fahmy Bey was shot by his wife. In 1924, Sir Lee Stack (the governor-general of Sudan) was assassinated in Cairo. In 1928, Arthur Mace, a member of the excavation team, died of arsenic poisoning. In 1929, Richard Bethell, Carter's secretary, was smothered in his bed. And in 1939, Howard Carter died from Hodgkin's disease. While the rumors of a curse became synonymous with Tutankhamun's tomb, no mention of a curse was ever found in the tomb, and many people who were involved with the excavation lived long and happy lives.

Chapter 14: Hatshepsut and Cleopatra: Women in Power

Ancient Egypt was ruled by many powerful individuals who changed the course of history. Two of those rulers were women who came to rule Egypt in their own right by using tricky political situations to their advantage. Hatshepsut and Cleopatra weren't the first women to rule Egypt, but they were able to hold onto the throne for many years and left a lasting influence. Although their reigns were unusual for the time period, they were both successful rulers who managed to endear themselves to their subjects. The success of their reigns can be attributed to their skill, ingenuity, and creative problem-solving.

Hatshepsut was the legitimate heir to the throne and proved her capabilities by ruling on behalf of her ineffectual husband. She was eventually able to rule in her own right and came up with a creative way to maintain the Egyptian principle of harmony and balance, which required both a male and female ruler on the throne. Cleopatra, on the other hand, had to outsmart her family and navigate her way through a deadly political situation to secure the throne. Unfortunately, both women had their reputations tarnished, and their legacy had been obscured by time, rumors, and vindictive successors and scholars.

Hatshepsut's Rise to Power

Hatshepsut was born around 1504 BCE to Thutmose I and his wife, Ahmose. It seems that Hatshepsut was extremely proud of her father and even reburied him in her own grand tomb. She also claimed that he named her as his successor before he passed, but this was unlikely since female pharaohs were unheard of at the time. Thutmose I was a capable king who expanded Egypt's borders. He was famous for his military campaigns and allegedly sailed home to Thebes after a successful Nubian campaign with the naked body of a Nubian chief hanging from his ship.

Traditionally, the throne was passed from the pharaoh to his son. Usually, the honor went to the pharaoh's son by his queen, but if the queen didn't have a son, then the son of a secondary wife (a concubine in the harem) would be chosen. Ahmose seems to have provided Thutmose I with two sons, but they both died early. As a result, Thutmose I's heir was Thutmose II, his son by one of his secondary wives, Mutnofret. In order to strengthen Thutmose II's lineage, he married Hatshepsut when she was only twelve years old. Sculptures depicting her as Thutmose II's wife show her standing behind her husband.

However, Thutmose II was weak and couldn't live up to his father's legacy. As the queen of Egypt, Hatshepsut was elevated to the position of God's Wife of Amun. During her marriage, Hatshepsut gave birth to Neferure, a daughter and Hatshepsut's only known child.

As the God's Wife of Amun, Hatshepsut played a role in policy-making and presided over Amun's festivals. Although not much is known about her exact responsibilities, it is likely that she would have played an important role in Egyptian society and been worshiped as a divine being. She would also have been required to sing and dance for Amun at all his festivals in order to get him to take part in them. Her role as the God's Wife of Amun would have exposed her to the inner workings of the government.

Thutmose II died around 1479 BCE, and the throne was passed to Thutmose III, the son of one of Thutmose II's secondary wives. Hatshepsut was appointed as the prince's co-regent and was only supposed to rule until he was old enough to take the throne. This was a common practice in Egypt, as widowed queens would usually rule on behalf of their younger male relatives until they were old enough to rule alone. Although Hatshepsut was definitely ruling the kingdom, Thutmose III was recognized as the king of Egypt.

All that changed in the seventh year of her regency. She declared herself the pharaoh of Egypt and took on all the pharaoh's titles. While she still used feminine grammatical terms when she inscribed her titles, she began depicting herself with the male pharaonic beard. Thutmose III was displaced. He was depicted in carvings with Hatshepsut but was usually smaller than her or placed directly behind her. It was clear who was truly ruling the kingdom.

Reign

Hatshepsut realized that she would have to be creative in order to strengthen her rule since she had no precedent to follow. One of her first acts was to marry her daughter, Neferure, to Thutmose III and make Neferure the God's Wife of Amun. Her actions ensured that even if she was somehow deposed, she would still be one of the most powerful people in all of Egypt. She also claimed that the god Amun had visited Ahmose one night and tricked the queen into believing he was Thutmose I. When the god revealed himself to the queen, she was overcome, and they conceived Hatshepsut. She also claimed that Thutmose I had appointed her as his co-regent and that her reign had been prophesied by an oracle some eighty years earlier.

Hatshepsut statues, portrayed on the right with the pharaonic beard.
JCarriker, uploaded by Giorces, CC BY 2.5 https://creativecommons.org/licenses/by/2.5
via Wikimedia Commons; https://commons.wikimedia.org/wiki/File:Hatshepsut.jpeg

Hatshepsut's efforts succeeded, and she was the first woman to rule Egypt in her own right. Sobekneferu likely ruled before Hatshepsut, but it is hard to know in what capacity due to the lack of information. Hatshepsut launched various military campaigns and began numerous construction projects. She also relied heavily on one of her advisors, Senenmut. The courtier attained astonishing influence during Hatshepsut's reign and was placed in charge of all her construction projects. He was also tasked with taking care of Neferure. Hatshepsut proved to be a capable leader who brought prosperity to the country. She fostered new trade routes and was even able to launch her own expedition to the neighboring Kingdom of Punt. According to records, she returned with boats loaded with ivory, myrrh trees, exotic animals, and gold. She considered the expedition to be her greatest achievement and had the event carved into the walls of her mortuary temple. It was such a success that her popularity and influence were greatly increased.

Hatshepsut's Building Projects

Hatshepsut put a lot of effort into legitimizing her reign, and one of the ways she strengthened her position was by building extensively. Her projects provided many jobs for the common people, and they were incredibly beautiful. The fact that she was able to complete so many projects shows that she was responsible for all of Egypt's resources, as she wouldn't have been able to complete any of them without access to significant wealth. It also attests to the fact that the country must have been at peace during her reign since she wouldn't have been able to divert that many resources if she had been preoccupied with defending her orders or invading other countries.

Temple of Hatshepsut.

She was able to expand the temple at Karnak and build her grand mortuary temple at Deir el-Bahari. Scholars have noted that her temples were elegantly constructed. Hatshepsut's mortuary temple featured courtyards of trees, pools, and a terrace. One of the terraces was lined with columns that led to another impressive terrace. Her burial chamber was at the back of the building and carved into the mountain itself. The temple was decorated with inscriptions, statues, and reliefs. Hatshepsut was one of the first to build in the Valley of the Kings, and her temple inspired future pharaohs to also build their temples in the valley. Hatshepsut was a great patron of the arts. She commissioned so many pieces that almost every museum featuring ancient Egyptian art has a piece that was commissioned by her.

For most of Hatshepsut's reign, Thutmose III served as a general in the Egyptian army. Around 1457 BCE, Thutmose III went on a campaign to suppress a rebellion in Kadesh, which became known as the Battle of Megiddo. When he returned, he became king, and Hatshepsut disappeared from the ancient records. Hatshepsut had likely died by that point. However, Thutmose III changed his regnal date to begin after the death of his father and took credit for all of Hatshepsut's accomplishments.

Cleopatra's Early Life

Cleopatra was born in 69 BCE and was named Cleopatra VII Philopator. Sometime during her youth, she became her father's co-regent. Cleopatra's father was Ptolemy XII Auletes, and her mother may have been Cleopatra V Tryphaena. In 51 BCE, Ptolemy XII died (likely of natural causes) and left eighteen-year-old Cleopatra the throne. Tradition dictated that she had to rule with a male counterpart, and she was married to her brother, Ptolemy XIII. However, she soon dropped his name from the official records and ruled in her own right.

Cleopatra proved to be a competent leader and a gifted polyglot. She was able to converse naturally in Egyptian, Greek, and several other languages. This allowed her to develop close relationships with diplomats. She was known for being charismatic. Plutarch reported that she personally worked with diplomats from "barbarian nations" without needing a translator. However, she soon caused friction with her own councilors since she often made decisions without consulting them. In 48 BCE, she was betrayed by her advisors when they led a coup against her and installed her brother on the throne. Cleopatra and her sister, Arsinoe, were forced to flee to safety.

Julius Caesar

Around this time, Pompey the Great (a Roman politician) was fighting against Julius Caesar. Pompey had spent a lot of time in Egypt and believed the Ptolemies were on his side. When he lost the Battle of Pharsalus, he fled to Egypt, hoping to gain sanctuary and support. As soon as he arrived in Alexandria, he was murdered on the shore, apparently as Ptolemy XIII watched. It's possible that Ptolemy XIII's chief advisor, Pothinus, advised the young king to murder Pompey, as it was believed that Julius's victory over Pompey was a sign of divine favor. Unfortunately for Ptolemy XIII, Julius Caesar was deeply offended by Pompey's murder. When he arrived in Alexandria, he declared martial law and made himself the interim ruler of Egypt, forcing Ptolemy XIII to flee to Pelusium.

Cleopatra welcoming Caesar.
https://commons.wikimedia.org/wiki/File:Cleopatra_welcoming_Caesar.jpg

When Cleopatra heard about the situation, she knew she had to gain favor with Julius Caesar. According to legend, Cleopatra rolled herself into an expensive rug and was carried into the palace. Julius Caesar was immediately smitten by the young woman, and the two became lovers. When Ptolemy XIII returned to his palace the next day, he found that Cleopatra had won over Caesar. As a result, war broke out between the Roman legions and the Egyptian army. During that time, Cleopatra and Caesar were forced to hide in the palace until Roman reinforcements arrived. The war took place in Alexandria, and the city was greatly damaged. More Roman soldiers arrived six months later, and their victory seemed inevitable. While Cleopatra likely felt secure in her position alongside Julius Caesar, she was about to be betrayed again, this time by the sister she had taken with her into exile.

Arsinoe

Sometime before the Roman victory, Arsinoe escaped from the palace and joined Ptolemy XIII. She was then proclaimed as the queen of Egypt in place of her older sister. This would have been a massive blow to Caesar's and Cleopatra's cause, as Ptolemy XII's will read that his successors would be his son and daughter, who ruled side by side. Arsinoe managed to turn the tide against the Romans and even trapped Caesar in a section of the city by blocking off certain streets. Afterward, her forces poured seawater into the Roman cisterns, which would have contaminated their freshwater supplies. Caesar attempted to launch an attack on the Lighthouse of Alexandria in an effort to gain the upper hand. Arsinoe's forces managed to trap him there, but he stripped off his armor and jumped into the harbor.

At one point during the war, Arsinoe was betrayed by her troops and given as a prisoner to Julius Caesar in exchange for Ptolemy XIII (who had been captured sometime during the fighting). Soon after, the Romans won the war, and Ptolemy XIII drowned in the Nile during a battle. In 46 BCE, Arsinoe was a part of Julius

Caesar's victory parade in Rome. According to Roman tradition, she was supposed to be executed after the procession, but she won sympathy from the Romans, and Julius Caesar was forced to spare her life. Instead of allowing her to return to Egypt, where she would pose a threat to Cleopatra's rule, she was sent to the Temple of Artemis at Ephesus, which was a famous sanctuary for political prisoners. Arsinoe was murdered in 41 BCE when Mark Antony commissioned assassins to kill her. She was dragged out of the Temple of Artemis and strangled on the steps, which caused a massive scandal in Rome. The temple sanctuary was supposed to be sacred, and the murder was seen as an obscene violation of Roman law.

Reign

After Julius Caesar won the war in Alexandria, he restored Cleopatra to the throne. She was joined by her younger brother, Ptolemy XIV, who was thirteen years old at the time. He chose to stay in Egypt along with Cleopatra, and the two of them toured extensively throughout Egypt as Cleopatra established her authority. In 47 BCE, Cleopatra gave birth to Caesar's son, Ptolemy Caesar (Caesarion), who became Cleopatra's heir. At this point, she began aligning her image with that of the mother goddess, Isis. Sometime around 45 BCE, Cleopatra traveled to Rome with Julius Caesar and remained there until Caesar was murdered in 44 BCE.

While Cleopatra was becoming popular in Egypt, she didn't gain much influence in Rome. Caesar had openly continued his relationship with Cleopatra despite being married to Calpurnia. He even publicly acknowledged that Caesarion was his son. The Romans had strict laws against bigamy, and Caesar's actions were highly unpopular. As a result, the Romans criticized Cleopatra harshly, and she gained few Roman allies. Sometime after Cleopatra returned to Egypt, Ptolemy XIV died (it's rumored that he was poisoned by Cleopatra), and Caesarion became Cleopatra's co-regent. At this point, she began representing herself as Isis and her son as Horus.

Mark Antony

After Julius Caesar was assassinated, Rome was plunged into a time of political chaos as the government tried to find a successor. Eventually, Mark Antony and Octavian emerged as Caesar's successors and became joint rulers of Rome. Mark Antony controlled the eastern part of the empire, while Octavian controlled the west. In 41 BCE, Antony summoned Cleopatra to Tarsus and planned to charge her with giving aid to Roman rebels. Cleopatra purposefully arrived late, and when she finally sailed into Tarsus, she presented herself as the goddess Aphrodite. She reportedly arrived in a gilded barge with purple sails and sat under a canopy made of golden cloth. Mark Antony was smitten with Cleopatra, and the two entered into a relationship that would last for ten years. During those years, Cleopatra gave birth to twins: Alexander Helios and Cleopatra Selene II. Mark Antony even divorced his wife, Octavia, and married Cleopatra.

Cleopatra sailing into Tarsus.
https://commons.wikimedia.org/wiki/File:Alma-tadema-antony-cleopatra.jpeg

Unfortunately, Mark Antony's relationship with Octavian eventually declined, and Rome was plunged into war. Mark Antony had lost support in Rome due to his flagrant disregard for Roman tradition. It certainly didn't help Mark Antony's case that he publicly humiliated Octavian's sister when he divorced her in favor of Cleopatra. Mark Antony and Cleopatra lost the Battle of Actium in 31 CE. A year later, they were forced to contend with the Roman army, which was set on invading Egypt. According to legend, Mark Antony stabbed himself after hearing that Cleopatra had been killed. Octavian reportedly allowed Mark Antony to be returned to Cleopatra, where he died in her arms. She committed suicide soon after, and Octavian would eventually become the sole Roman emperor. Unfortunately, Cleopatra's grand claims for Caesarion led to his execution, but her twins were allowed to continue living.

Chapter 15: Saladin: The First Sultan of Egypt

Saladin was the first sultan of both Egypt and Syria. His efforts founded the Ayyubid dynasty, and he was instrumental in unifying the medieval Muslim states, although his campaigns against other Muslim leaders earned him many enemies. During his peak, he ruled over Syria, Egypt, parts of Mesopotamia, western Arabia, Yemen, parts of North Africa, and Nubia.

Early Life

Saladin was born in Tikrit, Iraq, around 1137 CE. He was named Yusuf Ibn Ayyub and was part of a powerful military family. His father, Ayyub, and uncle, Shirkuh, served under the governor of northern Syria, Imad al-Din Zangi. Saladin's lineage would have exposed him to influential figures and given him the skills that he would later employ in his military campaigns. He grew up in Damascus and quickly proved his worth. Saladin gained a reputation for being an expert horseman and polo player. As a young man, he rose quickly through the military ranks and served under his uncle when they were sent on a military expedition to Egypt.

Shirkuh served under Zangi's son, Nur al-Din. In 1169, Shirkuh died, and Saladin was chosen to take his uncle's place. At that point, Saladin was appointed as a vizier to the Fatimid Caliphate. Two years later, the last Fatimid caliph died, and Saladin immediately proclaimed himself the governor of Egypt. The rulers of the Fatimid dynasty had been Shia Muslims, but Saladin was a Sunni Muslim. He immediately began curbing Shia influence. During his time as the Egyptian governor, he strengthened Egypt, and it became a powerful Sunni base. As vizier, Saladin began reforming the social and economic conditions in the kingdom. He eliminated taxes that were contrary to Islamic law and began building a powerful navy. Saladin still ruled in Nur al-Din's name; at the time, Nur al-Din was the governor of Aleppo and Edessa. However, Saladin began putting family members in positions of power within his government and pushed back against Nur al-Din's rule. Finally, Saladin's chance came in 1174 when Nur al-Din died. His successors immediately began fighting for dominance. The chaos provided Saladin with an opportunity to announce that he was the sultan of Egypt.

Sultan of Egypt

As soon as Saladin was in control of Egypt, he set his sights on a larger goal. He organized his state according to Islamic law and began removing Shiite influence in Egypt. This boosted his reputation and influence in the Muslim world, especially when he declared that he was the protector of the Sunni Orthodoxy. Saladin decided that he wanted to form a Muslim coalition, which would prove to be an extremely difficult task. The Muslim world was made up of highly independent states with their own rulers. Some of those states were made up of Shia Muslims, which meant that Saladin had to overcome regional and religious differences.

Sometime in 1174, he uncovered a plot to put the Fatimids back in power, and he dealt with the traitors in a swift and brutal manner. He also built several mosques and madrasahs in order to expand

Sunni influence within Egypt. His popularity among the Sunni Muslims grew, and he appointed Sunni Muslims to positions within the government and courts. Saladin allowed Egyptians to hold power within his government, which gave him insight into the traditions of the Egyptian populace. He was famously tolerant of other religions and allowed Coptic Christians and Jews to continue practicing their beliefs. During Saladin's reign, the Egyptian economy continued to flourish as it had during the Fatimid Caliphate.

Muslim Coalition

In 1174, Saladin managed to capture Damascus, which was an impressive feat. From there, he went on to conquer Aleppo, Mosul, and Yemen. He soon came to control the Red Sea region, which brought him one step closer to his ultimate goal. However, Saladin didn't simply rely on military methods to gain new territories. He was an adept diplomat who fostered strong relationships with other leaders, which gave him many allies. In order to establish the legitimacy of his rule, he married Nur al-Din's widow since she was the daughter of a previous ruler of Damascus. Saladin also won widespread respect in the Muslim world by taking the lead in the efforts to protect Islam against the invading Christians.

While Saladin proclaimed to be a protector of Islam, he had no problem fighting Muslim enemies. The caliph of Baghdad recognized most of Saladin's authority, but Aleppo remained beyond his reach. It was ruled by Nur al-Din's son, who proved to be a dangerous enemy. Saladin survived numerous attempts on his life. The Assassins, or the Nizari Ismailis, was a dangerous Muslim sect that held a number of forts in Persia and Syria. They were known for choosing prominent leaders and then sending small teams of highly skilled assassins to kill them. Saladin didn't take kindly to these attempts and promptly pillaged an Assassin castle in Masyaf, Syria. He finally managed to capture Aleppo in 1183 after using the Egyptian fleet. By 1186, Saladin was in control of Syria,

Palestine, and northern Mesopotamia, which allowed him to unify most of the Muslim world.

Holy War against Christianity

Saladin built up an impressive reputation and proclaimed that he was the only one who could win the war against the Crusaders. Throughout his reign, he met the Franks (what the Crusaders from Europe were called back then) in battle on a number of occasions. In 1177, he lost a battle to the Franks but managed to secure a small victory in 1179 at Marj Ayyun, where he was able to take hold of an important fortress on the Jordan River.

While Saladin set about unifying the Muslim world, he also sought to prove that he could expel the Franks from Muslim lands. However, he had to focus on strengthening his own lands first, as he couldn't successfully win the war if he was constantly checking his borders. This meant he had to be content with small battles until he could be certain that his own borders were secure. The Muslim coalition that he dreamed of was within his grasp, but it was also clear the coalition was somewhat fragile and would fall apart if he wasn't careful.

By 1187, Saladin could finally focus all his attention on the holy war. In May 1187, a force led by Saladin's son, al-Afdal, attacked Kerak Castle, which was held by the Franks. Meanwhile, Saladin gathered an army made up of troops from Aleppo, Jazira, Syria, and Egypt. The Franks were forced to mobilize their own forces, and the two armies met at Hattin.

Battle of Hattin

On July 3rd, 1187, Saladin's forces began the battle when his mounted archers repeatedly fired on the Franks, after which they would retreat and begin firing again. The Franks were forced to advance under near-constant attack. Saladin's army was made up of about twenty thousand men. The Franks were led by Guy of Lusignan, King of Jerusalem. (The Kingdom of Jerusalem was the

Frankish kingdom of Palestine. It was established in 1099 after the First Crusade.) The Franks had 15,000 troops and 1,300 knights. Saladin held the clear advantage with his larger army, but he also had a steady stream of supplies thanks to his camel trains. The Franks, on the other hand, were quickly running out of water.

Saladin and Guy of Lusignan
https://commons.wikimedia.org/wiki/File:Saladin_and_Guy.jpg

Saladin realized the Franks were dealing with thirst and ordered his men to set fire to the dry bush around the battlefield, which would have made the Franks unbearably thirsty. The Franks were desperate and had managed to assemble their biggest army ever, but they were quickly overcome by Saladin's forces. The Franks' formation fell apart, which allowed the Muslim forces to break through their lines and defeat the army. After the battle, Saladin famously offered his new captive, Guy of Lusignan, an iced sherbet. Saladin ransomed some nobles but executed hated nobles who had attacked or pillaged Muslim communities. He also executed some of the Knights Hospitaller and Knights Templar since they were extremely dangerous due to their fanaticism. The captives who couldn't be ransomed were sold as slaves.

In September 1187, Saladin finally managed to capture Jerusalem. The victory was extremely important, as Jerusalem was the symbolic prize for both religions. He either ransomed or sold the Western Christians into slavery. The Eastern Christians were allowed to remain, but most of their churches were turned into mosques. Saladin's victory at Hattin and Jerusalem turned him into a hero in the Muslim world. He successfully captured several other cities held by the Franks. Eventually, the Franks only held Tyre.

Third Crusade

The Crusaders suffered massive losses during Saladin's rule, and he made it clear that he intended to rid the Middle East of the Franks altogether. When Saladin captured Jerusalem, Pope Gregory II persuaded some of the most powerful kings in Europe to wage a holy war. Saladin was prepared for them; he also wanted to engage in a holy war, as this would finally bring an end to the Crusaders' presence. Three European kings responded to the pope's call, and soon, Richard I of England, Philip II of France, and Frederick I Barbarossa of the Holy Roman Empire and Germany were on their way to the Middle East.

Meanwhile, Guy of Lusignan began a siege on Acre in August 1189. When Philip and Richard's army arrived, the battle turned in favor of the Crusaders. They managed to capture the city in 1191, along with a large portion of Saladin's navy. From there, the Crusaders made their way to Jerusalem. In September 1191, the Crusaders and Muslims met at Arsuf and engaged in a large battle. The Crusaders won, and Saladin's reputation was greatly damaged due to his successive losses. Other Muslim leaders criticized Saladin's reluctance to attack Tyre when he had the chance, but Saladin's strategy had always been to attack an enemy where they were weak and wear them down. While the Crusaders marched toward Jerusalem, the Muslim army launched small-scale attacks and slowly wore down the Christian army. By the time the Crusaders arrived at Jerusalem, they were in no position to recapture the city. In 1192, Saladin agreed to a truce with Richard the Lionheart, which brought an end to the Third Crusade.

Reputation

During his lifetime, Saladin employed a number of talented biographers who helped boost his reputation as a generous, just, noble, and chivalrous leader. Saladin was also known for enjoying gardening and poetry. He was hailed as a hero in the Muslim world for his victories against the Crusaders. Saladin carefully cultivated his reputation as the ideal Muslim ruler who lived according to Islamic law and ruled fairly over conquered states. It must be noted that Saladin was famously tolerant of other religions and allowed Christians and Jews to live peacefully in his empire. He also chose not to massacre Christian populations when he recaptured the Franks' territory. Most Sunni historians gave Saladin enormous amounts of praise, and his reputation as a competent military leader and pious man would endure long after his death.

Christian writers were also positive in their descriptions of the Muslim conqueror. They portrayed him as a reasonable and generous man who allowed many Christians to go free. Medieval European societies placed a lot of emphasis on the value of chivalry and courtesy. Saladin was known for these qualities, which painted him as a worthy adversary to the Crusaders.

Death

The end of the Third Crusade and the departure of the Crusaders meant that Saladin had successfully won the holy war, which had been one of his most important goals. He had also managed to unify the Muslim states into a mighty empire. However, he died on March 4th, 1193, just a few months after his truce with Richard the Lionheart. He was around fifty-five years old. He likely died from fatigue or exhaustion caused by his extensive military campaigns. Unfortunately, his Muslim coalition wouldn't survive long after his death. Once Saladin died, his three sons took control of a portion of his empire, namely Egypt, Aleppo, and Damascus.

The rest of the empire was divided among other family members and high-ranking officials.

The Ayyubid dynasty continued to rule over Egypt and Syria but was overthrown by the Mamluks between 1250 and 1260. Saladin's reputation endured in Islamic and Christian literature, and he was upheld as an example of chivalry in Europe. The fact that his good reputation was maintained even after his empire disintegrated is a testament to the power he held during his lifetime.

Chapter 16: Mubarak and Morsi

Ancient Egyptian politics is usually a source of intense study and fascination, and rightly so because ancient Egypt was a remarkable empire. Modern Egyptian history is also worth observing since the country plays an important role in the worldwide economy. Two of the most important politicians in modern Egyptian history are Hosni Mubarak and Mohamed Morsi. Both of these men were highly influential politicians who left a definite mark on their country. They were both presidents during the 21st century and were often at the center of political controversy. Coincidentally, both were involved in a revolution that ended with their removal from the government.

Mubarak ruled for decades and was a seasoned politician before Egypt erupted into protests that called for his resignation. Morsi was an engineer who won Egypt's first democratic election but was removed from his position after a few months and forced to stand trial. People remain divided on their legacies, especially since Morsi died while being held in a detention center. There are a lot of theories and interesting stories about the men, which makes looking into their lives a worthwhile endeavor.

Hosni Mubarak: Early Life

Hosni Mubarak was born in Kafr El-Meselha, Monufia governate, Egypt, in May 1928 and joined the Egyptian military academy during his youth. He graduated in 1949 and received advanced flight and bomber training from the Soviet Union. Mubarak eventually earned a degree in aviation sciences and served in the Spitfire fighter squadron for two years. During his time in the Egyptian Air Force, he held several positions of power before becoming the director of the air academy. He was appointed as the chief commander of the air force and the deputy minister of defense in 1972 by President Anwar Sadat.

Mubarak played an important part in the war with Israel in 1973. At the beginning of the war, the Egyptian Air Force surprised the Israeli troops on the east bank of the Suez Canal. The attack was extremely successful, as the Egyptian pilots hit the vast majority of their targets. As a result of his military successes, Mubarak became very popular and was promoted to air chief marshal. The Egyptian Air Force played an important role in the war, and they proved to be a morale booster for Egyptian ground troops.

General Hosni Mubarak
https://commons.wikimedia.org/wiki/File:General_Hosni_Mubarak.jpg

In 1975, Sadat appointed Mubarak as his vice president.

Vice Presidency

As the vice president of Egypt, Mubarak played an important role in government consultations concerning the results of the war with Israel. He went on a mission to Riyadh and Damascus to discuss the disengagement agreement between Egypt and Israel. The aim of the mission was to persuade the Syrian and Saudi Arabian governments to accept the agreement. During this time, Mubarak fostered a friendship with Saudi Arabian Crown Prince Fahd. He also managed to make powerful friends with various other Arab leaders.

Sadat often sent Mubarak to consult with foreign leaders, so he was a regular part of sensitive government meetings. He played an important role in the negotiations of Middle Eastern policies. Mubarak was chosen to serve as a mediator during the dispute between Algeria, Morocco, and Mauritania over the fate of Western Sahara. Sadat made good use of Mubarak during his vice presidency, and it's clear that Mubarak used this time to make important allies.

President of Egypt

Anwar Sadat was assassinated on October 6th, 1981, during the anniversary celebrations of the Yom Kippur War. Mubarak was injured during the assassination but was still able to become the next president of Egypt. Due to Sadat's choice to negotiate a peace treaty with Israel, Egypt's membership was suspended from the Arab League since it didn't agree with Sadat's plan. When Mubarak became president, he entered into negotiations with King Fahd of Saudi Arabia. Egypt and Saudi Arabia were both powerful forces in the Arab world; Egypt was very populous, while Saudi Arabia was extremely rich. In 1982, Saudi Arabia presented an Egyptian peace plan that dictated Israel should resolve the Israeli-Palestinian conflict by ensuring the formation of a Palestinian state. In return, Israel would be at peace with the Arab world. During Mubarak's presidency, he fostered good relationships with the other Arab countries and the United States. He also reaffirmed the peace treaty with Israel as per the Camp David Accords, but he didn't have the same close relationship with Israel as his predecessor.

George W. Bush and Hosni Mubarak.
https://commons.wikimedia.org/wiki/File:President_George_W._Bush_and_Hosni_Mubarak.jpg

In 1987, Mubarak was elected to a second term. Mubarak supported the Saudi plan to invite the US military coalition to recover Kuwait during the Persian Gulf crisis and the ensuing war. By 1993, Mubarak was facing political unrest from opposing political parties that wanted to usher in new democratic electoral reforms in Egypt. The unrest led to guerilla warfare. Mubarak condemned the actions of the Islamic fundamentalists after an attack at Luxor in 1997 that killed sixty tourists. For most of his presidency, he was a vocal supporter of peace in the Middle East.

Mubarak faced assassination attempts in 1995 and 1999, with the second attempt leaving him slightly wounded. In 1999, he was reelected as president since he ran unopposed. In 2005, Egypt's first multi-candidate presidential election took place, although it was plagued by reports of inconsistencies and low voter turnout. Unsurprisingly, Mubarak was reelected to another term.

Revolution and Overthrow

In 2011, Egypt was gripped by widespread protests against Mubarak's presidency, which was beset by rising poverty and allegations of corruption and repressive policing tactics. The protestors called for Mubarak's resignation, and the police clashed violently with the protestors. Millions of Egyptians protested against Mubarak, calling for his immediate resignation. During the revolution, 846 people were killed, and over 6,000 were injured. On January 28th, Mubarak gave a speech announcing he had no intention of resigning; however, he intended to introduce political change by dissolving his cabinet. He also promised to instigate other political and social changes, but his promises did little to stop the protestors. In order to gain the protestors' trust, Mubarak appointed the first vice president of his presidency, Omar Suleiman. He then announced he wouldn't take part in the Egyptian presidential elections in September 2011.

Egyptian protests (January 25th, 2011).
*Adam Makary, CC BY-SA 2.0 https://creativecommons.org/licenses/by-sa/2.0 via Wikimedia Commons;
https://commons.wikimedia.org/wiki/File:Egyptian_Revolution_protests_(25_January_201 1)_-_03_-_Flickr_-_Al_Jazeera_English.jpg*

On February 10ᵗʰ, 2011, Mubarak gave Suleiman some of his duties, but instead of resigning immediately as the protestors wanted, he declared he would remain as president until the end of his term. He also claimed that he would reform the electoral system. The next day, he left for his house in the Sinai Peninsula. On that same day, Suleiman addressed the nation and told the people that Mubarak had stepped down and left the Supreme Council of the Armed Forces in control of the government. The announcement led to celebrations in Tahrir Square and other urban centers.

Death

After Mubarak was forced from his position, the government began cracking down on former officials and business leaders accused of corruption or abuse of power. Soon, there were calls to investigate the former president, as the Mubarak family had been accused of stealing money from the state and hiding it in foreign accounts. Mubarak's sons, Alaa and Gamal, were investigated. Mubarak denied the serious accusations that he and his family were facing. On April 12ᵗʰ, he reportedly suffered a massive heart attack that caused him to be held in a hospital in Sharm el-Sheikh. It was determined that the former president was too weak to be transferred to a prison.

In May, it was announced that Mubarak would stand trial for abuses of power and ordering the killing of protestors during the revolution. Mubarak attended his trial in a hospital bed and denied all the charges. In January 2012, it was announced that the prosecutors intended to seek the death penalty for the former president. In June of that year, the court declared that Mubarak had been complicit in the deaths of the protestors. He was sentenced to life in prison. He was acquitted of the corruption charges, but in January 2013, the court announced that Mubarak had to be retried for corruption and the killings of the protestors. Later in the year, he was transferred to a military hospital in Cairo. In 2014, Mubarak received a three-year sentence for embezzling public funds, while his sons received a four-year sentence. However, the court later dismissed the charges that Mubarak was responsible for the deaths of the protestors. In January 2020, Mubarak was admitted to the hospital for surgery but died in February at the age of ninety-one.

Mohamed Morsi: Early Life

Mohamed Morsi was born in the Al-Sharqiyyah governate in Egypt on August 8th, 1951. He came from a humble background; his father was a farmer, and his mother was a housewife. In the 1960s, he began studying at Cairo University and received a bachelor's in engineering with high honors. In 1976, he completed his military service in the Egyptian Army, where he served in the chemical warfare unit. Once he finished his military service, he returned to Cairo University, where he earned a master's in metallurgical engineering in 1978. He also earned a scholarship that allowed him to complete his studies in the United States, where he received a PhD in materials science from the University of Sothern California. When he returned to Egypt, he became a professor at Zagazig University.

Mohamed Morsi.

Morsi became a member of parliament in 2000. He was a member of the Guidance Office of the Muslim Brotherhood and served as an independent candidate in parliament, as the Muslim Brotherhood was banned from running for government. In 2011, the Muslim Brotherhood founded the Freedom and Justice Party, and Morsi became the first president of it. He condemned the two-state solution of the Israel-Palestine conflict, condemned the 9/11 attacks, and criticized the United States for invading Afghanistan and Iraq after the attacks. His views were supported by many Egyptians, but he was harshly criticized by his enemies. Morsi was arrested during the protests in January 2011 but managed to escape prison.

President of Egypt

After Mubarak resigned, the Freedom and Justice Party was allowed to run for election. In April 2012, Morsi became the party's candidate. He was the party's second choice, but his predecessor, Khairat al-Shater, was disqualified. Morsi won the election; however, the interim military government made a constitutional declaration in June that essentially took away most of the president's authority. The Supreme Constitutional Court also dissolved the People's Assembly, which was led by the Muslim Brotherhood. Regardless, Morsi was sworn into office on June 30th.

As president, Morsi reversed the interim military government's constitutional declaration, and several members of the council retired at the same time. In November 2012, Morsi helped negotiate a ceasefire between Israel and Hamas (a Palestinian Sunni-Islamic fundamentalist militant and nationalist organization) in the Gaza Strip, which earned him international praise. However, he later issued a decree that stipulated his authority wouldn't be subject to any judicial oversight until a permanent constitution was established. The decree took away the court's ability to monitor the Constituent Assembly, which was responsible for coming up with a new constitution. This move led to widespread protests, with the Egyptians claiming that Morsi was making himself a dictator.

In the midst of the protests, Morsi took back some of his decrees, although he kept the decree that prevented the removal of the Constituent Assembly. The Constituent Assembly had created a draft constitution, which was made by Muslims without input from Christian or secular members. In December, Morsi declared martial law, which allowed the military to arrest anyone whom they deemed as a threat, and the draft constitution was approved by voters. Morsi faced overwhelming opposition during his term, and many of his opponents weren't open to negotiations, which forced the president to take drastic measures.

Overthrow and Trial

Morsi's presidency was plagued by worsening political situations, a decline in public services, and a weakening economy. These failures drew harsh criticism, and by June 30th, 2013, anti-Morsi protests were taking place throughout the country. The protests grew steadily out of control, and soon, there were calls for his removal. In July, the head of the Egyptian Armed Forces, General Abdel Fattah al-Sisi, decided to take decisive action. He announced that unless Morsi was able to placate the protestors, the military would be forced to step in and prevent the country from descending into anarchy.

Morsi's situation was becoming more precarious by the day. Morsi offered to negotiate with the protestors but declared that he wouldn't resign from his post. He rejected the military's ultimatum and declared that he would find his own way to reconcile the nation.

Anti-Morsi protests in Tahrir Square.
*Y. Weeks/VOA, Public domain, via Wikimedia Commons;
https://commons.wikimedia.org/wiki/File:Thousands_of_people_gather_in_Tahrir_Square
_to_protest_Egyptian_President_Mohamed_Morsi_-_30-Nov-2012.jpg*

Two days later, the military removed Morsi from his post and suspended the constitution. Morsi and many of his Muslim Brotherhood colleagues were put in prison. Morsi's supporters erupted into protests over his removal, especially since Morsi's supporters were being repressed. In July and August, the military clashed violently with the protestors. More than one thousand protestors were killed, with most of the deaths taking place at Rabaa al-Adawiya Square. In September, the Muslim Brotherhood was outlawed again. Al-Sisi then left the military and became the Egyptian president in 2014.

Morsi was forced to stand trial for inciting Muslim Brotherhood supporters to kill protesters during an anti-Morsi protest and for colluding with foreign groups, such as Hamas and Iran's Revolutionary Guards. During his trial, Morsi declared that the allegations were false and that he was still the rightful president of Egypt. The proceedings were widely denounced and criticized.

Death

In April 2015, Morsi was found guilty of inciting violence against anti-Morsi protestors and sentenced to twenty years in prison. He was also charged with conspiring to commit acts of terrorism in Egypt and was sentenced to life in prison. On top of this, he was sentenced to death for committing violence during a mass prison break in January 2011. In 2016, an Egyptian court ordered a retrial and overturned the death sentence. While the new trial began, Morsi was kept in jail. Unfortunately, the conditions were deplorable, and he wasn't allowed access to adequate medical attention. The prison conditions led to Morsi's poor health, and on June 17th, 2019, he collapsed in court and died.

In response, the United Nations called for an independent inquiry into Morsi's death. Mosques all around the world gave special prayers for the former Egyptian leader. Many foreign governments denounced the coup and blamed the Egyptian government for Morsi's death. The Muslim Brotherhood claimed that Morsi wasn't allowed to receive regular visits from allies or family members and that Morsi wasn't provided with necessary medicine. Apparently, the details of his health had been kept secret.

The Freedom and Justice Party held the Egyptian government responsible for Morsi's "deliberate and slow death." They claimed that Morsi was placed in solitary confinement, fed disgusting food, and not given basic human rights. His allies also called for an independent international investigation into Morsi, saying the results should be made available to the public. Mohamed Morsi was buried by his family in Al-Wafaa Wa al-Amal cemetery in Cairo. So far, this independent investigation has not happened, but it might still happen in the future.

Conclusion

Egypt is an alluring country that draws millions of tourists to view its spectacular historical sights. The country has endured climactic changes that threatened its security and transformed its social, religious, and economic structures. Each of these changes brought about a new era in Egyptian history and had a profound effect on the country and its neighbors. This book provided a general overview of Egypt's history and took a look at ancient, medieval, and modern events that left a mark on Egypt's identity.

We explored ancient Egypt and the age of pyramids and pharaohs. We saw how Egypt was irrevocably changed when Alexander the Great arrived on the scene. When he died, his vast empire was divided among his heirs, and Ptolemy I seized his chance to take over Egypt. During this time, Egypt was heavily impacted by the Hellenistic culture, and Alexandria became an intellectual powerhouse in the Mediterranean. The Ptolemies were responsible for building legendary monuments, such as the Library of Alexandria and the Lighthouse of Alexandria.

Eventually, Egypt became a Roman province and later formed a vital part of the Byzantine Empire. By then, Christianity was well established in Egypt and had become the state religion. During the medieval period, Egypt was invaded by the Rashidun Caliphate, which established Islam as the new state religion. Egypt was ruled by various Muslim rulers, including the Abbasids, the Fatimids, the Mamluks, and the Ottomans. Each ruling dynasty left its mark on Egyptian art and architecture, which led to the complex diversity that still dominates the modern Egyptian landscape.

Egypt is a magnificent country with a powerful history that will be studied for years to come. By learning more about its past, a person can broaden their knowledge about some of the most important events in world history.

Here's another book by Enthralling History
that you might like

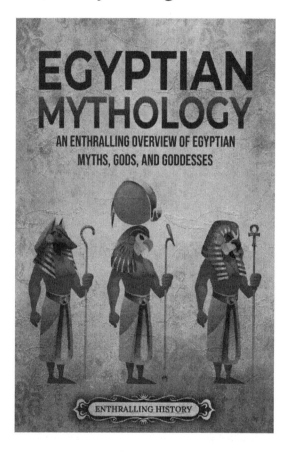

Free limited time bonus

Stop for a moment. We have a free bonus set up for you. The problem is this: we forget 90% of everything that we read after 7 days. Crazy fact, right? Here's the solution: we've created a printable, 1-page pdf summary for this book that you're reading now. All you have to do to get your free pdf summary is to go to the following website: **https://livetolearn.lpages.co/enthrallinghistory/**

Once you do, it will be intuitive. Enjoy, and thank you!

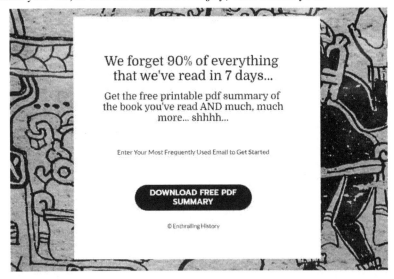

We forget 90% of everything
that we've read in 7 days...

Get the free printable pdf summary of
the book you've read AND much, much
more... shhhh...

Enter Your Most Frequently Used Email to Get Started

**DOWNLOAD FREE PDF
SUMMARY**

© Enthralling History

Bibliography:

Title: Who were the mysterious Neolithic people that enabled the rise of ancient Egypt? Here's what we've learned on our digs

  Link: https://theconversation.com/who-were-the-mysterious-neolithic-people-that-enabled-the-rise-of-ancient-egypt-heres-what-weve-learned-on-our-digs-121070

  Date Accessed: 12/4/22

Title: Upper Egypt

  Link: https://www.britannica.com/place/Upper-Egypt

  Date Accessed: 12/4/22

Title: Lower Egypt

  Link: https://www.britannica.com/place/Lower-Egypt

  Date Accessed: 12/4/22

Title: Narmer

  Link: https://www.worldhistory.org/Narmer/

  Date Accessed: 12/4/22

Title: Old Kingdom of Egypt

Link:
https://www.worldhistory.org/Old_Kingdom_of_Egypt/

Date Accessed: 12/4/22

Title: Djoser

Link: https://www.worldhistory.org/Djoser/

Date Accessed: 12/4/22

Title: First Intermediate Period of Egypt

Link:
https://www.worldhistory.org/First_Intermediate_Period
_of_Egypt/

Date Accessed: 12/4/22

Title: The Great Pyramids of Giza

Link: https://www.khanacademy.org/humanities/ap-art-
history/ancient-mediterranean-ap/ancient-egypt-ap/a/old-
kingdom-the-great-pyramids-of-giza

Date Accessed: 12/4/22

Title: Snefru

Link: https://www.britannica.com/biography/Snefru

Date Accessed: 12/4/22

Title: Imhotep

Link: https://www.worldhistory.org/imhotep/

Date Accessed: 12/4/22

Title: Horus

Link: https://www.britannica.com/topic/Horus

Date Accessed: 12/4/22

Title: Seth

Link: https://www.britannica.com/topic/Seth-Egyptian-god

Date Accessed: 15/4/22

Title: Isis

Link: https://www.britannica.com/topic/Isis-Egyptian-goddess

Date Accessed: 15/4/22

Title: Middle Kingdom of Egypt

Link: https://www.worldhistory.org/Middle_Kingdom_of_Egypt/

Date Accessed: 15/4/22

Title: Mentuhotep II

Link: https://www.britannica.com/biography/Mentuhotep-II

Date Accessed: 15/4/22

Title: Ancient Egypt's Middle Kingdom Period

Link: https://www.thoughtco.com/ancient-egypt-middle-kingdom-period-118155

Date Accessed: 15/4/22

Title: Amenemhet I

Link: https://www.britannica.com/biography/Amenemhet-I

Date Accessed: 15/4/22

Title: Senusret III

Link: https://www.worldhistory.org/Senusret_III/

Date Accessed: 15/4/22

Title: Amenemhet III

Link: https://www.britannica.com/biography/Amenemhet-III

Date Accessed: 15/4/22

Title: Sebeknefru

Link: https://www.britannica.com/biography/Sebeknefru

Date Accessed: 15/4/22

Title: Turin Papyrus

Link: https://www.britannica.com/topic/Turin-Papyrus

Date Accessed: 18/4/22

Title: New Kingdom of Egypt

Link: https://www.worldhistory.org/New_Kingdom_of_Egypt/

Date Accessed: 19/4/22

Title: Hyksos

Link: https://www.worldhistory.org/Hyksos/

Date Accessed: 19/4/22

Title: No one expected this pharaoh to found Egypt's most powerful dynasty

Link: https://www.nationalgeographic.com/culture/article/ahmose-i

Date Accessed: 19/4/22

Title: Hatshepsut

Link: https://www.worldhistory.org/hatshepsut/

Date Accessed: 19/4/22

Title: Thutmose III: The Napoleon of Ancient Egypt

    Link: https://discoveringegypt.com/ancient-egyptian-kings-queens/thutmose-iii-the-napoleon-of-ancient-egypt/

    Date Accessed: 19/4/22

Title: Amenhotep III

    Link: https://www.worldhistory.org/Amenhotep_III/

    Date Accessed: 19/4/22

Title: Akhenaten

    Link: https://www.livescience.com/39349-akhenaten.html

    Date Accessed: 19/4/22

Title: Tutankhamun

    Link: https://www.britannica.com/biography/Tutankhamun

    Date Accessed: 19/4/22

Title: Ramses I

    Link: https://www.britannica.com/biography/Ramses-I

    Date Accessed: 19/4/22

Title: Ramesses II

    Link: https://www.worldhistory.org/Ramesses_II/

    Date Accessed: 19/4/22

Title: Ramses III

    Link: https://www.britannica.com/biography/Ramses-III

    Date Accessed: 19/4/22

Title: The Rise of the Ramessides: How a Military Family from the Nile Delta Founded One of Egypt's Most Celebrated Dynasties

> Link: https://www.arce.org/resource/rise-ramessides-how-military-family-nile-delta-founded-one-egypts-most-celebrated
>
> Date Accessed: 19/4/22

Title: The Cult of Amun

> Link: https://www.archaeology.org/issues/174-1505/features/3146-sudan-nubia-dangeil-cult-of-amun-ra
>
> Date Accessed: 21/4/22

Title: Third Intermediate Period of Egypt

> Link: https://www.worldhistory.org/Third_Intermediate_Period_of_Egypt/
>
> Date Accessed: 21/4/22

Title: Egypt from 1075 BCE to Macedonian Invasion

> Link: https://www.britannica.com/place/ancient-Egypt/Egypt-from-1075-bce-to-the-Macedonian-invasion
>
> Date Accessed: 21/4/22

Title: Nubian Pharaohs of Twenty-Fifth Dynasty Egypt

> Link: https://www.thoughtco.com/nubian-pharaohs-wenty-fifth-dynasty-egypt-3989880
>
> Date Accessed: 21/4/22

Title: Late Period of Ancient Egypt

> Link: https://www.worldhistory.org/Late_Period_of_Ancient_Egypt/
>
> Date Accessed: 21/4/22

Title: Alexander in Egypt and Some Consequences

Link: https://www.jstor.org/stable/3853895?read-now=1&refreqid=excelsior%3Aa4de2b1b0f39bc3a48400199287264b9&seq=1

Date Accessed: 21/4/22

Title: Esarhaddon and Egypt: An Analysis of the First Invasion of Egypt

Link: https://www.jstor.org/stable/43074609?read-now=1&refreqid=excelsior%3A02412609704e33c923c78df7b5939f7d&seq=1

Date Accessed: 21/4/22

Title: Alexander the Great Egypt History

Link: https://www.journeytoegypt.com/en/blog/alexander-the-great

Date Accessed: 21/4/22

Title: The Battle of Pelusium: A Victory Decided by Cats

Link: https://www.worldhistory.org/article/43/the-battle-of-pelusium-a-victory-decided-by-cats/

Date Accessed: 21/4/22

Title: Ptolemaic Dynasty

Link: https://www.worldhistory.org/Ptolemaic_Dynasty/

Date Accessed: 21/4/22

Title: Ptolemy I

Link: https://www.worldhistory.org/Ptolemy_I/

Date Accessed: 21/4/22

Title: Hellenic Culture in Egypt

Link: https://www.jstor.org/stable/3853691

Date Accessed: 21/4/22

Title: Roman Egypt

    Link: https://www.worldhistory.org/Roman_Egypt/

    Date Accessed: 21/4/22

Title: Cleopatra

    Link: https://www.britannica.com/biography/Cleopatra-queen-of-Egypt

    Date Accessed: 21/4/22

Title: The Battle of Actium

    Link: https://www.history.com/this-day-in-history/the-battle-of-actium

    Date Accessed: 21/4/22

Title: Vespasian

    Link: https://www.britannica.com/biography/Vespasian

    Date Accessed: 21/4/22

Title: Diocletian

    Link: https://www.worldhistory.org/Diocletian/

    Date Accessed: 21/4/22

Title: Egypt's role in the Byzantine Empire

    Link: https://www.britannica.com/place/ancient-Egypt/Egypts-role-in-the-Byzantine-Empire

    Date Accessed: 21/4/22

Title: Bubonic Plague Traced to Ancient Egypt

    Link: https://www.nationalgeographic.com/science/article/bubonic-plague-traced-to-ancient-egypt

    Date Accessed: 29/4/22

Title: Egypt from the Islamic Conquest to 1250

    Link: https://www.britannica.com/place/Egypt/From-the-Islamic-conquest-to-1250

    Date Accessed: 29/4/22

Title: Rashidun

    Link: https://www.britannica.com/topic/Rashidun

    Date Accessed: 29/4/22

Title: Islamic Egypt Time-line

    Link: https://www.ucl.ac.uk/museums-static/digitalegypt/chronology/islamic.html

    Date Accessed: 29/4/22

Title: The Abbasid Empire

    Link: https://courses.lumenlearning.com/atd-herkimer-worldcivilization/chapter/the-abbasid-empire/

    Date Accessed: 29/4/22

Title: Fatimid Dynasty

    Link: https://www.britannica.com/topic/Fatimid-dynasty

    Date Accessed: 29/4/22

Title: The Ottoman Conquest of Egypt (1517) and the Beginning of the Sixteenth-Century World War

    Link: https://www.jstor.org/stable/162225?read-now=1&refreqid=excelsior%3Ae70bd594a54955011cfd60ba9e33c592&seq=1

    Date Accessed: 29/4/22

Title: Sasanian dynasty

    Link: https://www.britannica.com/topic/Sasanian-dynasty

    Date Accessed: 29/4/22

Title: Post- Byzantine Egypt

    Link: https://courses.lumenlearning.com/suny-hccc-worldcivilization/chapter/post-byzantine-egypt/

    Date Accessed: 2/5/22

Title: Mamluks

    Link: https://www.newworldencyclopedia.org/entry/Mamluks

    Date Accessed: 2/5/22

Title: Egyptian Views of Ottoman Rule: Five Historians and Their Works, 1820-1920

    Link: https://read.dukeupress.edu/cssaame/article-abstract/31/1/149/59700/Egyptian-Views-of-Ottoman-Rule-Five-Historians-and

    Date Accessed: 3/5/22

Title: The Ottomans (1517-1798)

    Link: https://www.britannica.com/place/Egypt/The-Ottomans-1517-1798

    Date Accessed: 3/5/22

Title: The Campaign in Egypt

    Link: https://www.napoleon.org/en/history-of-the-two-empires/articles/the-campaign-in-egypt/

    Date Accessed: 3/5/22

Title: Napoleon's military defeat in Egypt yielded a victory for history

    Link: https://www.nationalgeographic.co.uk/history-and-civilisation/2021/01/napoleons-military-defeat-in-egypt-yielded-a-victory-for-history

    Date Accessed: 3/5/22

Title: Battle of the Nile

> Link: https://www.britannica.com/event/Battle-of-the-Nile

> Date Accessed: 3/5/22

Title: Ottoman Empire

> Link: https://www.history.com/topics/middle-east/ottoman-empire#:~:text=Decline%20of%20the%20Ottoman%20Empire,-Starting%20in%20the&text=In%201683%2C%20the%20Ottoman%20Turks,the%20Ottoman%20Empire%20in%201830.

> Date Accessed: 3/5/22

Title: Biography of Suleiman the Magnificent, Sultan of the Ottoman Empire

> Link: https://www.thoughtco.com/suleiman-the-magnificent-195757

> Date Accessed: 3/5/22

Title: From the French to the British occupation (1798-1882)

> Link: https://www.britannica.com/place/Egypt/From-the-French-to-the-British-occupation-1798-1882

> Date Accessed: 3/5/22

Title: The Nature of Plague in Late-Eighteenth Century Egypt

> Link: https://www.jstor.org/stable/44448549

> Date Accessed: 3/5/22

Title: The Ottoman Response to the Egyptian Crisis of 1881-82

> Link: https://www.jstor.org/stable/4283219

> Date Accessed: 3/5/22

Title: Muhammed 'Ali

> Link: https://rpl.hds.harvard.edu/faq/muhammad-%E2%80%98ali
>
> Date Accessed: 3/5/22

Title: Icelandic Volcano Caused Historic Famine in Egypt, Study Shows

> Link: https://www.sciencedaily.com/releases/2006/11/061121232204.htm
>
> Date Accessed: 3/5/22

Title: Abbas II

> Link: https://www.britannica.com/biography/Abbas-II-khedive-of-Egypt
>
> Date Accessed: 3/5/22

Title: WWI in Egypt: A forgotten sacrifice for colonial powers

> Link: https://egyptindependent.com/wwi-egypt-forgotten-sacrifice-colonial-powers/#:~:text=Egypt%20was%20drawn%20in%20the,the%20residents%20of%20the%20city.
>
> Date Accessed: 3/5/22

Title: Egypt

> Link: https://courses.lumenlearning.com/boundless-worldhistory/chapter/egypt/
>
> Date Accessed: 3/5/22

Title: Wafd

> Link: https://www.encyclopedia.com/history/asia-and-africa/egyptian-history/wafd
>
> Date Accessed: 3/5/22

Title: Saad Zaghloul

Link: https://www.britannica.com/biography/Saad-Zagloul

Date Accessed: 3/5/22

Title: World War II and its aftermath

Link: https://www.britannica.com/place/Egypt/World-War-II-and-its-aftermath

Date Accessed: 3/5/22

Title: Gamal Abdel Nasser elected president of Egypt

Link: https://www.history.com/this-day-in-history/nasser-elected-president

Date Accessed: 3/5/22

Title: What is the Muslim Brotherhood

Link: https://www.aljazeera.com/features/2017/6/18/what-is-the-muslim-brotherhood

Date Accessed: 3/5/22

Title: Egypt: from revolution to coup to crisis, a timeline

Link: https://www.trtworld.com/africa/egypt-from-revolution-to-coup-to-crisis-a-timeline-37581

Date Accessed: 3/5/22

Title: Egypt President Abdul Fattah al-Sisi: Ruler with an iron grip

Link: https://www.bbc.com/news/world-middle-east-19256730

Date Accessed: 3/5/22

Title: Anwar Sadat

> Link: https://www.britannica.com/biography/Anwar-Sadat
>
> Date Accessed: 5/5/22

Title: Social Structure in Ancient Egypt

> Link: https://www.worldhistory.org/article/1123/social-structure-in-ancient-egypt/
>
> Date Accessed: 5/5/22

Title: Ottoman Cairo

> Link: https://www.laits.utexas.edu/cairo/history/ottoman/ottoman.html
>
> Date Accessed: 5/5/22

Title: Clothing and Adornment

> Link: https://www.historymuseum.ca/cmc/exhibitions/civil/egypt/egcl06e.html
>
> Date Accessed: 5/5/22

Title: Ancient Egyptian Law

> Link: https://www.worldhistory.org/Egyptian_Law/
>
> Date Accessed: 5/5/22

Title: Who were the Mamluks?

> Link: https://www.historytoday.com/miscellanies/who-were-Mamluks
>
> Date Accessed: 5/5/22

Title: Roman Egypt

> Link: https://www.metmuseum.org/toah/hd/regy/hd_regy.htm
>
> Date Accessed: 5/5/22

Title: Roman and Byzantine Egypt: background information

    Link: https://www.ucl.ac.uk/museums-static/digitalegypt/roman/background.html

    Date Accessed: 5/5/22

Title: The Ptolemaic Dynasty

    Link: https://www.khanacademy.org/humanities/whp-origins/era-3-cities-societies-and-empires-6000-bce-to-700-c-e/36-the-growth-of-empires-betaa/a/read-the-ptolemaic-dynasty-beta

    Date Accessed: 5/5/22

Title: Society in the Byzantine Empire

    Link: https://www.worldhistory.org/article/1214/society-in-the-byzantine-empire/#:~:text=Byzantine%20society%2C%20as%20in%20that,were%20an%20even%20lower%20category).

    Date Accessed: 5/5/22

Title: Social Structure of the Ottoman Empire

    Link: https://www.thoughtco.com/social-structure-of-the-ottoman-empire-195766#:~:text=People%20associated%20with%20the%20Ottoman,members%20of%20the%20other%20professions.

    Date Accessed: 5/5/22

Title: Christian Monks and Muslim Villagers in medieval Egypt: A Library of Congress Story

    Link: https://blogs.loc.gov/kluge/2019/06/christian-monks-and-muslim-villagers-in-medieval-egypt-a-library-of-congress-story/

    Date Accessed: 5/5/22

Title: Medieval Muslim Societies

Link: https://www.khanacademy.org/humanities/world-history/medieval-times/social-institutions-in-the-islamic-world/a/medieval-muslim-societies#:~:text=Muslim%2Dmajority%20and%20Muslim%2Druled,by%20smaller%2C%20decentralized%20regional%20powers.

Date Accessed: 5/5/22

Title: Why the Nile River Was So Important to Ancient Egypt

Link: https://www.history.com/news/ancient-egypt-nile-river#:~:text=The%20Nile%2C%20which%20flows%20northward,the%20midst%20of%20a%20desert.

Date Accessed: 6/5/22

Title: Impact of the Nile River on Ancient Egypt

Link: https://pages.vassar.edu/realarchaeology/2017/04/09/impact-of-the-nile-river-on-ancient-egypt/

Date Accessed: 6/5/22

Title: The Nile and Egyptian Religion

Link: https://courses.lumenlearning.com/atd-fscj-earlyhumanities/chapter/the-nile-and-egyptian-religion/

Date Accessed: 6/5/22

Title: Nilus

Link: https://www.greekmythology.com/Other_Gods/Minor_Gods/Nilus/nilus.html

Date Accessed: 6/5/22

Title: Ancient Egyptian Mythology

Link: https://www.worldhistory.org/Egyptian_Mythology/

Date Accessed: 6/5/22

Title: Hapi

Link: https://www.britannica.com/topic/Hapi

Date Accessed: 6/5/22

Title: Plant and Animal Life

Link: https://www.britannica.com/place/Nile-River/Plant-and-animal-life

Date Accessed: 6/5/22

Title: Quest for the Source of the Nile

Link:
https://earthobservatory.nasa.gov/images/7236/quest-for-the-source-of-the-nile#:~:text=Beginning%20in%20the%20mid%2D1800s,the%20Nile's%20%E2%80%9Ctrue%E2%80%9D%20source.

Date Accessed: 6/5/22

Title: The Nile's Source Discovered

Link:
https://www.historytoday.com/archive/nile%E2%80%99s-source-discovered#:~:text=John%20Hanning%20Speke%20discovered%20the,Nile%20on%20August%203rd%2C%201858.&text=John%20Hanning%20Speke%2C%20an%20army,at%20the%20age%20of%20seventeen.

Date Accessed: 6/5/22

Title: The Ancient Egyptian Economy

Link: https://rosenlearningcenter.com/article/689/the-ancient-egyptian-economy?username=rosensample&password=rosensample#:~:text=Agriculture%20made%20up%20a%20major,papyrus%2C%20stone%2C%20and%20gold.

Date Accessed: 6/5/22

Title: Oceanus' Family

Link:
https://www.greekmythology.com/Titans/Oceanus/ocean
us.html

Date Accessed: 6/5/22

Title: Khnum

Link: https://www.britannica.com/topic/Khnum

Date Accessed: 6/5/22

Title: Ancient Egyptian Religion

Link: https://courses.lumenlearning.com/suny-hccc-
worldcivilization/chapter/ancient-egyptian-
religion/#:~:text=The%20religion%20of%20Ancient%20
Egypt,control%20the%20forces%20of%20nature.

Date Accessed: 6/5/22

Title: Egyptian Gods- The Complete List

Link: https://www.worldhistory.org/article/885/egyptian-
gods---the-complete-list/

Date Accessed: 6/5/22

Title: The Emergence of Christianity in Egypt

Link: https://dailynewsegypt.com/2013/06/19/the-
emergence-of-christianity-in-egypt/

Date Accessed: 6/5/22

Title: Christian Cairo

Link:
https://www.laits.utexas.edu/cairo/history/babylon/babylo
n.html

Date Accessed: 6/5/22

Title: History of Egypt from the 7th Century

    Link: https://www.introducingegypt.com/modern-history

    Date Accessed: 6/5/22

Title: Jewish Life in Ancient Egypt

    Link:
https://www.brooklynmuseum.org/opencollection/exhibitions/752#:~:text=Jews%20lived%20peacefully%20among%20the,its%20lack%20of%20ethnic%20tensions.

    Date Accessed: 6/5/22

Title: Serapis

    Link: https://www.worldhistory.org/Serapis/

    Date Accessed: 6/5/22

Title: The Cult of Alexander at Alexandria

    Link: https://www.jstor.org/stable/263514

    Date Accessed: 6/5/22

Title: Islam in Egypt

    Link: https://rpl.hds.harvard.edu/faq/islam-egypt

    Date Accessed: 6/5/22

Title: Diocletian, Persecution Of

    Link:
https://www.encyclopedia.com/religion/encyclopedias-almanacs-transcripts-and-maps/diocletian-persecution

    Date Accessed: 6/5/22

Title: Fatimids Caliphate

    Link:
https://www.newworldencyclopedia.org/entry/Fatimids_Caliphate

    Date Accessed: 6/5/22

Title: What's The Difference Between Sunni and Shi'a
Muslims

Link: https://crestresearch.ac.uk/comment/whats-
difference-sunni-shia-
muslims/#:~:text=Sunnis%20focus%20on%20following
%20the,parts%20of%20the%20Middle%20East.

Date Accessed: 6/5/22

Title: Byzantine Egypt and the Coptic Period, an Introduction

Link: https://smarthistory.org/egypt-coptic-period-
introduction/

Date Accessed: 7/5/22

Title: 8 Facts About Ancient Egypt's Hieroglyphic Writing

Link: https://www.history.com/news/hieroglyphics-facts-
ancient-egypt

Date Accessed: 7/5/22

Title: Tombs

Link:
https://www.historymuseum.ca/cmc/exhibitions/civil/egy
pt/egca02e.html#:~:text=The%20first%20royal%20tomb
s%2C%20called,that%20have%20long%20since%20disa
ppeared.

Date Accessed: 7/5/22

Title: Pyramids at Giza

Link:
https://www.nationalgeographic.com/history/article/giza-
pyramids

Date Accessed: 7/5/22

Title: Inside the Tombs of Saqqara

Link: https://www.smithsonianmag.com/history/inside-tombs-saqqara-180977932/

Date Accessed: 7/5/22

Title: Uncovering Secrets of the Sphinx

Link: https://www.smithsonianmag.com/history/uncovering-secrets-of-the-sphinx-5053442/

Date Accessed: 7/5/22

Title: Ancient Egyptian Fortresses

Link: https://weaponsandwarfare.com/2018/09/20/ancient-egyptian-fortresses/

Date Accessed: 7/5/22

Title: The New Kingdom

Link: https://courses.lumenlearning.com/boundless-arthistory/chapter/the-new-kingdom/#:~:text=There%20are%20six%20great%20temples,sandstone%20from%20south%2Dwestern%20Egypt.

Date Accessed: 7/5/22

Title: Copt

Link: https://www.britannica.com/topic/Copt

Date Accessed: 7/5/22

Title: The Transition from Coptic to Arabic

Link: https://journals.openedition.org/ema/1920

Date Accessed: 7/5/22

Title: Discovering the wonder of Egypt's Islamic architecture

Link: https://www.arabnews.com/node/1044981/art-culture

Date Accessed: 7/5/22

Title: Akhenaten

Link: https://www.worldhistory.org/Akhenaten/

Date Accessed: 7/5/22

Title: Tutankhamun

Link: https://www.history.com/topics/ancient-history/tutankhamen

Date Accessed: 7/5/22

Title: How Did King Tut Die?

Link: https://www.history.com/news/king-tut-death-mystery

Date Accessed: 7/5/22

Title: Ay

Link: https://www.britannica.com/biography/Ay-king-of-Egypt

Date Accessed: 7/5/22

Title: Howard Carter

Link: https://www.britannica.com/biography/Howard-Carter

Date Accessed: 7/5/22

Title: The Discovery of King Tut's Tomb

Link: https://www.thoughtco.com/tomb-of-king-tut-discovered-1779242

Date Accessed: 7/5/22

Title: Archaeologist opens tomb of King Tut

Link: https://www.history.com/this-day-in-history/archaeologist-opens-tomb-of-king-tut

Date Accessed: 7/5/22

Title: Tutankhamun's Curse?

Link: https://www.historytoday.com/archive/months-past/tutankhamuns-curse

Date Accessed: 7/5/22

Title: Horemheb

Link: https://www.britannica.com/biography/Horemheb

Date Accessed: 9/5/22

Title: Tutankhamun

Link: https://www.britannica.com/biography/Tutankhamun

Date Accessed: 9/5/22

Title: Smenkhkare

Link: https://www.britannica.com/biography/Smenkhkare

Date Accessed: 9/5/22

Title: Ankhesenamun

Link: https://www.britannica.com/biography/Ankhesenamen

Date Accessed: 9/5/22

Title: Desperately Seeking Queen Nefertiti

Link: https://www.nationalgeographic.com/adventure/article/150814-nefertiti-tomb-tutankhamun-tut-archaeology-egypt-dna

Date Accessed: 9/5/22

Title: The Queen Who Would Be King

>Link: https://www.smithsonianmag.com/history/the-queen-who-would-be-king-130328511/

>Date Accessed: 9/5/22

Title: Who was Hatshepsut?

>Link: https://www.nationalgeographic.com/culture/article/hatshepsut

>Date Accessed: 9/5/22

Title: Hatshepsut

>Link: https://www.history.com/topics/ancient-history/hatshepsut

>Date Accessed: 9/5/22

Title: Hatshepsut

>Link: https://www.worldhistory.org/hatshepsut/#:~:text=Hatshepsut%20(r.,her%20stepson%20Thutmose%20III%20(r.

>Date Accessed: 9/5/22

Title: Cleopatra

>Link: https://www.history.com/topics/ancient-history/cleopatra

>Date Accessed: 9/5/22

Title: Arsinoe IV (D. 41 BCE)

>Link: https://www.encyclopedia.com/women/encyclopedias-almanacs-transcripts-and-maps/arsinoe-iv-d-41-bce

>Date Accessed: 9/5/22

Title: Cleopatra: Biography of the last pharaoh of ancient Egypt

> Link: https://www.livescience.com/44071-cleopatra-biography.html

> Date Accessed: 9/5/22

Title: Cleopatra

> Link:
> https://www.worldhistory.org/Cleopatra_VII/#:~:text=Cleopatra%20VII%20(l.%20c.%2069%2D30,of%20Alexander%20the%20Great%20(l.

> Date Accessed: 9/5/22

Title: Saladin

> Link: https://www.britannica.com/biography/Saladin

> Date Accessed: 10/5/22

Title: Saladin

> Link: https://www.history.com/topics/africa/saladin

> Date Accessed: 10/5/22

Title: Saladin

> Link: https://www.worldhistory.org/Saladin/

> Date Accessed: 10/5/22

Title: The Assassins

> Link: https://www.worldhistory.org/The_Assassins/

> Date Accessed: 10/5/22

Title: Why does Saladin have such good PR in the Medieval West?

> Link: https://www.medievalists.net/2014/09/saladin-good-pr-medieval-west/

> Date Accessed: 10/5/22

Title: Hosni Mubarak

> Link: https://www.britannica.com/biography/Hosni-Mubarak
>
> Date Accessed: 10/5/22

Title: Hosni Mubarak, Egyptian Leader Ousted in Arab Spring, Dies at 91

> Link: https://www.nytimes.com/2020/02/25/world/africa/hosni-mubarak-dead.html
>
> Date Accessed: 10/5/22

Title: Egypt's former President Hosni Mubarak dies at 91

> Link: https://www.aljazeera.com/news/2020/2/26/egypts-former-president-hosni-mubarak-dies-at-91
>
> Date Accessed: 10/5/22

Title: Mohamed Morsi

> Link: https://www.britannica.com/biography/Mohamed-Morsi
>
> Date Accessed: 10/5/22

Title: Mohamed Morsi, Who Brought the Muslim Brotherhood to the Egyptian Presidency

> Link: https://www.newyorker.com/news/news-desk/mohamed-morsi-who-brought-the-muslim-brotherhood-to-the-egyptian-presidency
>
> Date Accessed: 10/5/22

Title: Mohamed Morsi

> Link: https://www.aljazeera.com/tag/mohamed-morsi/
>
> Date Accessed: 10/5/22

Title: Mohamed Morsi's death: World Reaction

Link: https://www.aljazeera.com/news/2019/6/18/mohamed-morsis-death-world-reaction

Date Accessed: 10/5/22

Title: Italian Invasion of Egypt in WWII

Link: https://about-history.com/italian-invasion-of-egypt-in-wwii/

Date accessed: 28/6/22

Printed in Great Britain
by Amazon